Christine was born in Lancashire, and lives there today with her family. Her interests are dogs and animals in general, arts and crafts, and antiques. She has a distinction in canine studies, and took part in a canine aggression course. Christine is interested in dog welfare and the relationship between human and dog.

In writing this book, she hopes it will be an enjoyable read, and give a better understanding of the behaviour of dogs.

Christine Cornforth

IN THE DOG HOUSE

Vanguard Press

VANGUARD PAPERBACK

© Copyright 2016
Christine Cornforth
Illustrated by Alan Cornforth

A CIP catalogue record for this title is
available from the British Library.

ISBN 978 178465 1 602

Vanguard Press is an imprint of
Pegasus Elliot MacKenzie Publishers Ltd.
www.pegasuspublishers.com

First Published in 2016

Vanguard Press
Sheraton House Castle Park
Cambridge England

Printed & Bound in Great Britain

To family and friends
Human and Canine
Past and Present

In the Dog House

As a child, my home was a three-storey terraced cottage, formally a cottonmill worker's home in the small Lancashire village of Dolphinholme. My mother's family had lived in and around the village for generations.

Our household consisted of my mum and dad, my grandmother, my older sister, and me. At that time, in the 1960s, the village population was just beginning to become transient. It appeared that people from the nearby city of Lancaster had discovered Dolphinholme, and so began the commuter culture, which thrives in the village today.

In years gone by, it was usual for just the male members of the average family to be in employment, and, with most families, the female members only going out to work until they were married. In the countryside, the kind of employment some people were involved in also became a major part of their lifestyle, and I assume this was so with a number of my male ancestors. They were employed as gamekeepers, water bailiffs, groom, and farmers.

I know very little about my father's family, just that my dad was a soldier, and so was his father before him – my granddad. So, I think it must be the influence of ancestors in my mother's family who are mostly responsible for my love of animals and their welfare.

In the 1960s, it was common place for people in our village to open the door in the morning and let the family dog out, who would then wander freely around a small area surrounding their home and always returning by the evening. There were no physical restraints, such as being fenced in or tied up, but the dogs knew their boundaries. This meant that most dogs were very sociable, more so than some dogs today, although I most certainly am not suggesting that people today do that. Times have changed, and it would be dangerous in a number of ways, not to mention totally irresponsible for anyone to do so now. Anyway, my first memory of a dog is Tony. He lived next door but one to us and everyone in our row of cottages knew him. I found out later in life, Tony was a Shetland Sheepdog. He never wandered far, up to the top of our row of cottages and back was his territory, but mostly he stayed between his own home and mine.

Tony with my sister, Gill, and me in my Sooty & Sweep dress.

During the summer months, I was allowed to play out on the concrete at the back of our cottage, providing I didn't play in front of anyone else's house that was. Tony would come and join in my games, and sometimes I used to just sit on the back step with my arm around him, talking to him – and he always listened. I was about four years old at the time and remember asking my parents for a dog of our own. Any dog would do; at that time I had no idea about the different breeds – to me they were all brilliant, and I wanted one!

It seemed to me that no amount of pleading and promising to do anything my parents asked of me was getting me any closer to a dog of our own but it didn't stop me imagining what it would be like to have a dog in our family.

Every summer my mum worked on one of the local farms, picking potatoes. Not many farms had machinery to do this job in the 1960s so it provided annual casual work for a number of the village women. Each morning, they waited outside the village shop, which was at one end of our row of cottages, for someone from the farm to pick them up in a Land Rover.

This particular summer my mum came home from the farm one day and I noticed she was holding something inside her jacket. Mum called me to her asking, "what do you think of this?" You can imagine the smile on my face when she brought her hand out from her jacket and in her hand was a small black furry bundle, a puppy!

What a surprise; fancy my parents keeping a secret like that from me, even with all my pestering they didn't let on what they had got planned. One of the farm dogs had given birth to four puppies, and my mum had brought one home for us! I can still recall the feeling of excitement as Mum handed the puppy over to me, that sweet soft puppy smell filling my nostrils as I cuddled our new family member, Skippy, as we later named her. (Skippy, the bush kangaroo, was a popular children's TV programme at that time). A cross-bred dog, Skippy's mum was a terrier, and I'm not sure what her father was, but

11

maybe he was something like a Labrador, or a collie. Skippy fulfilled all my expectations of having a dog in the family. I hadn't started school then but my sister being eighteen months older than me had to go to school each weekday, so that left me with plenty of one-to-one time with our puppy to make that special bond whilst playing our games together. I knew that in the not too distant future, I too would have to go to school, but for now I had a puppy all to myself. My sister Gill, our dog Skippy, and I all grew up together. Skippy certainly played a major part in our childhood – she came out to play with us as well as also played games inside on rainy days besides accompanying us on our annual two week holiday to the seaside.

Milko

Skippy was very sociable and had made friends with our local milkman, Mr. Wilson. If I remember rightly, Mr. Wilson arrived at our house somewhere between eight thirty and nine every morning except Sundays. He also had a dog named Brandy – I think he was a Golden

Retriever – who always accompanied Mr. Wilson on his round. The milk van was always parked at the end of the road next to the two rows of terraced cottages. Mr. Wilson used to then walk up and down, backwards and forwards as need be, delivering his milk and collecting the empty bottles, with Brandy following at his heels.

In summer, our back door was always wide open from morning until night, and Mr. Wilson plus his dog Brandy would walk right into the kitchen with a cheerful good morning. Mr. Wilson put the bottles of milk down on the kitchen table where my mum also left the empties for him to pick up. Skippy always greeted Brandy and because it was something that had always happened she never felt threatened about the other dog entering her home. It was obvious that the dogs liked each other and Skippy being the youngest learned from Brandy's good behaviour, so it only seemed natural when Skippy was old enough she too accompanied Mr. Wilson and Brandy on their round, from our house onwards. This arrangement went on until Mr. Wilson's retirement, and I'm sure Skippy must have missed him and Brandy, who are certainly characters from my childhood who I remember with fondness.

At about age six, I was given a book about popular breeds of dog. Well that did it – from then on, I periodically pestered my parents about getting a Great Dane – well actually, I always asked for two! Since that time, it has been the Great Dane, who has fuelled my interest for all things canine.

Mud sticks

Later on in my teenage years, Skippy accompanied me, my friend Ena, and her dog Tess on many walks around the countryside of our childhood, although I don't think she got on as well with Tess as she did with Brandy. There were never any growls or snaps at each other but both Tess and Skippy seemed to tolerate each other rather than becoming companions. Tess was a Wirehaired Fox Terrier with attitude, and Skippy was a crossbred who knew she was every bit as good as a pedigree dog. One afternoon, close to Christmas Ena and Tess came to our house as we had arranged a woodland walk that afternoon. Tess had been bathed, clipped and brushed that morning and was looking every inch the pedigree dog she was. As we reached the woods, we took the route known locally as the Cinder Path, it is fairly straightforward and runs along the edge of the wood on one side, and a field which the River Wyre runs through on the other side, it's a spot you never tire of. Alongside the Cinder Path on the woodland side runs a small ditch. Both dogs were off lead, and a few steps in front of us, enjoying the afternoon investigating the trees shrubs and bushes. Tess suddenly stopped still looking into the woodland as if she had heard something – I must admit she did look particularly smart after her grooming session; instantly, Skippy ran to Tess's side and pushed her body against Tess's, who then fell plop into the little stream. Skippy just stood there looking at Tess and then at me as if she had intended to ruin Tess's new hair-do! Tess very quickly scrambled out of the ditch, although looking very different from the well-groomed dog who had set out on the walk with us. Her white fluffy fur was now covered in mud, and bits of twigs and dead leaves had managed to tangle themselves in her curly wire coat. She looked as if she had been living on the streets. We knew Tess wasn't hurt and I apologised for Skippy's actions, but being teenage girls we couldn't help but have a good giggle. It's a good thing that Ena's parents saw the funny side too although Ena was the one given the job of washing Tess down.

I have many happy memories of the time shared with Skippy, she reached the grand old age of eighteen, and like all the dogs who are no longer with us, I still miss her.

As I grew up, my interest in dogs grew too, and wherever I went I always took notice of the dogs around me – what breed they were, could I identify them, how did they behave, did they work, if so, what job were they intended for, were they sporting or were they pets. Large, small, long hair or short, the diverseness of the canine species had certainly captured my interest.

At nineteen, I was married and moved to another village some miles away. Fortunately, for me, my husband had a dog. She was an English Bull Dog and her name was Charlotte. Alan, my husband, told me that she had been given to him by a local breeder who no longer had any use for her. Apparently, she had been kept as a brood bitch, but unfortunately, she wasn't very maternal and when she had her first litter of puppies, no amount of coaxing or expert handling could encourage her to look after her babies. That meant Charlotte was not viable to a professional breeder, so instead they found her a new home. I think when I met Charlotte she was about five or six years old – a lovely girl, she just wanted to be part of the family. I think for a Bull Dog she was fairly fit and loved the outdoors; however, the characteristic squashed up nose of the breed meant that her breathing was impaired, which in turn had an effect on her mobility. Charlotte was born in the late 1970s and although to me, her breathing was better than that of some members of the same breed today, my reason for writing this down is because I believe some changes should be made to various breed standards for a number of the breeds of dog recognised by the Kennel Club.

Although I recognise there has to be some guidelines as to how certain breeds appear, I believe a dog should be judged primarily for its overall natural health and well-being, both physically and mentally. In my opinion, some breed characteristics listed in various breed standards disable the dog, rather than enhance the breed.

One evening, I arrived home after visiting my parents, to find another dog in the house. There was a young Dalmatian dog curled up on the hearthrug in front of the fire. Alan had also been out visiting some friends of his who had taken in this Dalmatian, who seemed to be getting passed around. They didn't want to keep the dog so he was brought to our house. Although I was thrilled to see George – as we later called him – I knew he hadn't been helped with any kind of training or basic life skills. I thought he was probably about ten or eleven months old, and he was very boisterous, just as a dog of that age should be. With this in mind, and the fact that I was heavily-pregnant, I realised this wasn't the best time for me or the dog to enter into this kind of relationship. Our intention was to find him the right kind of new home. George hadn't been house-trained when he came to us so that was at the top of the list. I worked with him as you would a new puppy, because to George everything was happening for the first time. Every time George had a wee-wee or a pooh-pooh outside in the garden, I said the appropriate word, praised him, and gave him a cuddle. Every chance I got, I took George into the garden and encouraged him to go to the loo. Within two weeks, he had greatly improved, and only had the odd accident on the kitchen floor. He had now been with us a number of weeks and soon the time for my baby being born grew ever closer. With that brought more thought to George's plight. I would have loved him to be part of our family but I knew I wasn't being fair to him if I kept him at that moment in time. Because of his less than ideal start in life, he needed someone who would be able to give him what he needed – time, patience, and understanding. I knew I wouldn't be able to give him time. So, the search was on to find a suitable family for George. Fortunately, for George it was discovered that some friends of the family would love to give a home to a Dalmatian. A meeting was arranged and the family and George hit it off. Although it was very upsetting, and with great reluctance, I let George go with his new family. I know it was the right thing to do for him. The good thing was, because he had gone to friends of the family, we got to know how well he was doing. During the week, George made regular appearances at the primary school where the lady of the family worked as a teacher, then most weekends in the summer, George spent relaxing in the lake district. It's satisfying knowing that he lived his life knowing he was loved very much, and had all the comforts a dog could wish for.

When our son Mark, was born, I usually took an afternoon walk; as I pushed the pram, Charlotte walked on her lead at my side. As Mark grew, the pram was swapped for a buggy. I always put my hand through the loop on the lead and held onto the push bar at the back of the buggy with my hands. Charlotte walked by Mark's side, never becoming distracted by anything we came across. Because Charlotte stayed by Mark's side, he was able to grasp her lead with his tiny hand. I never encouraged Mark to do this, it just happened naturally. It was something Mark just did, and Charlotte was always happy to be in Mark's company, and always stayed close to his side.

Country aroma

One evening, Alan and I went to the village pub and took Charlotte along with us. She enjoyed going to the pub for an hour or so because people always made a fuss of her. This particular evening was no different, and the pub was very busy. It was Blackpool illumination season, and because our village was on the way there, coach parties stopped to have a drink at the pub on the way there, then stopped on the way back at the local fish and chip shop. We sat at a table enjoying our drinks, and Charlotte was sat at Alan's side. Presently, the most awful smell drifted into my nostrils, I looked at Alan and smiled, I could see by the look on his face he knew as well as I did what was happening. The smell was getting stronger, it was like rotten eggs, cabbage, and a dung heap all rolled into one. Suddenly, the lady who was sat by the table to the back of us stood up shouting, 'oh no – not again', 'I thought I told you about that', 'you smelly article get out'. It seemed the woman was blaming the rotten smell on her teenage son.

The boy protested his innocence, stood up and pointed to Charlotte. "It's that dog there," he said.

"Don't you go blaming that little dog," his mother said. At this point Alan said that it was Charlotte.

"Oh no, it wasn't," the woman said, and carried on to say her son had been doing that all day, just to annoy the rest of the family, and she was sorry that he had blamed our dog. As she carried on telling her son off, we thought we had better take Charlotte home, before she caused any more trouble for the boy – we knew once she had started, there would be a few more to come!

Charlotte was growing older, and although she remained a very important member of the family, we decided it was time to give a home to a new puppy. One Saturday morning, when Mark was four years old, Alan, Mark, and myself, travelled to our local R.S.P.C.A. centre.

We didn't tell Mark of our intentions, until we arrived at the car park for the centre. As we got out of the car, I noticed the distinct smell of animals, and the noise of the dogs barking seemed to be coming from every corner of the building. We were met by a kennel worker who showed us into one of the smaller kennel buildings, in which the puppies were housed. There were three puppies available for adoption, and between the three of us, we chose a tiny black female pup. She was bouncing around, how puppies do and was eager to meet us all. Mark's face was a picture as the little pup chased the toy he had just thrown for her. Peggy, as Mark named the pup, soon settled into her new home with us. She was always eager to please, but of course there were the usual things you would expect of a puppy, like chewing shoes, paper, or anything else she came across including the telephone wire. We hadn't had any calls for a couple of days before we realised that one!

Peggy wasn't really any trouble though, even toilet training was easy. As a youngster, she did like digging in the garden though, and it could get quite frustrating when you had spent the afternoon planting up a new border, only to find when you had been indoors for a nice cup of tea, that Peggy had decided she didn't like the way you had positioned them so had removed them one by one, then scattered most of them all over the garden, keeping just a few back to hold in her mouth as she charged round the garden as if she was on a race track!

Mark had just started infant school when Peggy came into our lives, so when Peggy was old enough and had been given all her inoculations, I took her to meet Mark outside school at home time; most of the children were enchanted by her. Mark and Peggy grew up together, just has I had done with Skippy. They too had many happy hours together playing games and exploring the countryside around them.

As my son reached his teens, the Great Dane thing had come to the forefront of my mind again. My childhood friend Ena suggested that I contacted the Great Dane Rescue whom I could find out about via the Kennel Club.

Rupert: my first Great Dane

On telephoning the Kennel Club, I was given the number of a rescue worker, about sixty miles away from my home. When I telephoned the person at the rescue, we had a lengthy conversation, with me virtually giving my life story. I was told there was nothing in at the moment. They don't have kennels full of Great Danes but what they do is when they are called upon for assistance, they house the dog somewhere local to them, assess the dog's character and temperament, then try to make a match with the most suitable person they may have on their list.

Three months later, one evening, I received a telephone call. The rescue co-ordinator asked me if I was still interested – I could hardly get the word 'Yes' out quick enough!

I was told of a fawn dog called Rupert who was in rescue for the third time in his life. It was explained to me that he was a lovely friendly dog, but unfortunately, all the families he had gone to in the past had met with unforeseen circumstances beyond their control, and subsequently, all had been unable to keep him. Apparently, Rupert's last family had owned a pet shop but unfortunately, they had fallen on hard times. As so many others had done in the early 1990s, they had split up, with neither being able to take Rupert with them, leaving him homeless once again.

We arranged for us – my family – to go and meet the dog a few days later on a Saturday. When that day finally arrived, my husband Alan, son Mark, Peggy dog, and I, all set out early. It seemed to take ages to get there, but the drive was really nice as we made our way over the Peak District. We had arranged to meet the rescue co-ordinator at her home, and from there, she took us to a local boarding kennel, which was taking care of a number of Great Danes who were handed over to the rescue. Walking through reception and out into the kennel yard, the sound of various-sized dogs met our ears. As we approached the last isle, the Great Dane who was in the middle run, got to his feet and walked towards the front of the run. He obviously recognised the rescue co-ordinator who was with us, and knew there would be a treat in her hand, for him – a scone. Rupert was everything I had wished for – he was rich fawn in colour, with a small white patch on his chest, and a black mask covered his face, although that was now turning grey.

Given that the life span of the Great Dane is said to be about eight or nine years, it was feasible that Rupert could be about five or six. I asked the rescue co-ordinator if she knew Rupert's age, but she didn't. I couldn't believe my luck, I'd got just what I wanted – a lovely friendly Great Dane.

Our meeting went well, and I could see that my family were just as happy as I was, and although Rupert hadn't ever met us before, he was interested in us, and I knew then, we were going to get on.

I told Rupert everything would be all right, and that all we wanted was to love him. The next step would be to introduce Rupert to Peggy. This happened on neutral ground, by that I mean somewhere that neither dog considered to be their territory. The rescue co-ordinator suggested a nearby patch of ground, that she said was usually quiet, and such introductions had taken place there before. Being just across the road from the kennel she walked Rupert across, and after we had parked the car in a suitable place I clipped Peggy's lead on, she was keen to get out of the car to stretch her legs and have a sniff around. She noticed Rupert approaching, and stood there wagging her tail, they met nose-to-nose, sniffing and wagging tails. After walking around together for a few minutes, I indicated to both dogs to get in the car, this they did with no problem – we were on our way home. Canine introductions should always be undertaken on neutral ground – away from home – so that the existing resident dog doesn't feel that the new dog is encroaching on his or her territory as that could lead to conflict.

Dogs are sociable creatures, and usually get on with each other, providing the initial introduction is done properly, and theses two were no exception.

Anyone thinking of taking on a rescue dog of any kind should seriously consider it first. You must remember this is a time of stress for the dog. They have no idea who you are or what is going to happen to them, or for that matter why they had to leave their home. In my opinion, it can take many months for a rescue dog to settle in properly. After all, a bond has been broken between them and their original human companion and a new one needs to be built with you. Trust has to be earned – how does the dog know he/she is not going to be moved on again and how do they know you will care for them properly.

Dogs are taken into rescue for a number of reasons. They may have been ill-treated, and therefore could need special carers, but many are brought in due to marriage break ups, bankruptcies, owners not being able to cope, bereavement, or even unwanted gifts, for example. Rupert was probably cared for in his previous homes, and if it wasn't for the unfortunate and uncontrollable circumstances his previous families had found themselves in, he would not have been in a rescue situation.

Peggy and Rupert

Rupert was a fully-grown mature male, when he joined our household, it seems strange recalling this now, but the only way I can describe it is; it was certainly unusual, getting used to such a big dog in the house. He could stand at the back of the sofa, and rest his head on it, and his head was higher than my kitchen worktops, in fact, his body was bigger than mine!

It's probably something you don't really notice if you start off with a puppy, but you certainly do when your first Dane is a mature adult male! Having said that I never found the size to be a problem – just different, and I don't notice it now. Of course, related expenses are higher, e.g. vet bills, food, equipment, but you get something very special in return.

Rupert and Peggy were always together, and although Rupert was a lot bigger than Peggy, it was Peggy who was in charge, I feel this made

Rupert feel secure, and after all considering his unfortunate history, he must have felt relief. He settled in well, and became a much-loved member of our household.

As he got to know and trust us, his mischievous, playful character, began to shine through, and his sense of fun has given us many happy, cherished memories.

We spent many happy hours together, and I began to know and understand the breed, that I had admired for so long. Rupert's stay with us, was sadly all too short – Just under two years later, we lost him to *wobblers*. Or should I say – cervical vertebral instability. The first sign is usually uncoordinated or drunken like movements, usually in the hindquarters. With Rupert, I began to notice loss of strength in his hind legs, when out for walks he would periodically sit down, there didn't appear to be any reason for it, but it was totally out of character, although that seems quite contradictory when you consider that, when he was running free, he could run and jump just as well as always.

I took Rupert to the vet but was told it was just a sit down protest; I said it wasn't – well you know your own dog, don't you?

Further investigation was done, but came up with nothing – I don't know if they tested for *wobblers*, well I hadn't even heard of it then, and at that time certainly didn't know how it was tested. Rupert's problems were escalating, and I was desperately trying to get him some help. There were a number of visits to the vet, and each time Rupert showed no symptoms whilst at the surgery - I felt as though the vets thought it was me who had something wrong! They treated me as if I was making something out of nothing, and was just looking for attention – it was so frustrating, I just couldn't make them understand what was happening. I told the vets it seemed like Rupert's hind legs didn't belong to him, they would kind of sway, and maybe crossover each other, sometimes he would stumble - and as anyone who has experience of dogs knows, they are generally sure footed. Then there was the loss of feeling. Well I can only describe it as that, as Rupert couldn't tell me, could he. I felt his symptoms were escalating. On occasions, Rupert stubbed his toes, only it's as if he didn't know, he just carried on like nothing had happened, he didn't even lick his toes later – he couldn't feel it.

I don't think the loss of feeling was resigned to his legs and feet though, because on many occasions he would defecate and not know he was doing it. Whether he was lying down, or walking along, it just happened and he didn't notice, again that is something totally out of character for a dog, as we all know, dogs squat and get themselves into the right position before defecation.

There were also a couple of instances where Rupert appeared to be disorientated; I feel he found these to be quite unnerving, and I always tried my best to reassure him. I held him, and didn't leave his side, all the time trying to comfort him with the sound of my voice. When Rupert was like this, I didn't even know if he could tell it was me there, his eye's seemed to glaze, and he looked ahead of him, but I wasn't sure he could see. After each episode, Rupert was tired, but after resting, he was fine again.

I also noticed he began to have trouble turning his neck, it didn't move as far as it used to. By this time, I really was beginning to wonder if it was me – seeing things that weren't there, or maybe exaggerating. You see I was lacking in self-confidence, and had put my trust in the vet's – well they were the professionals, and who was I to say they were wrong. Now of course with age and experience, I would never let that situation occur.

Eventually Rupert went off his legs completely, and couldn't stand up at all; I called the vets again, this time it was someone new, who had just recently qualified. She knew right away what the problem was, and told me she had studied the disease at university. Rupert was diagnosed with *wobblers*, and was euthanized in early December 1995. I hadn't come across this disease before, and just felt helpless - and ignorant. I found his death difficult to cope with. I couldn't eat properly for weeks, frequently burst into tears, and was generally unhappy – I felt I had let him down.

In life, Great Danes create such a presence, that when they're no longer around, they leave behind a gaping hole so big; it's difficult to pull yourself out. I decided to find out more about canine medical problems, and how to deal with them. From there I changed my veterinary practice, and I am very happy with my current vets.

Hugo

It was only a matter of weeks since we had sadly lost Rupert, when I received a telephone call from a Great Dane rescue co-ordinator.

I was told there was a young male Great Dane, who was in desperate need of a home. The dog in question had been brought into rescue some months beforehand, by a young couple who had bought him as a puppy.

They had apparently chosen the largest puppy in the litter, and had no previous experience as dog owners with any kind of dog, but had thought that seeing as they had paid a substantial sum for their puppy, he would be well behaved. From then the dog had been re-homed twice, with both families bringing him back to rescue, saying they couldn't do anything with him, and that he was destroying their homes.

I agreed to go and meet the dog a couple of days later. The journey was about seventy to eighty miles each way, so it was to be an all day job. Peggy, our now twelve-year-old crossbreed loved this – she thought days out to be the best thing ever. She was confident in most situations, and eased the way for any new animal that came to live with us, whether it was dogs, cats, rabbits, or hens, Peggy made sure they felt safe in their new home. It was normal to see dogs, rabbits, and hens, all enjoying the same patch of land, under Peggy's careful supervision.

On arrival, my husband Alan, son Mark, Peggy, and I were shown into the office at the kennels where the young dog was being cared for.

We were told that he was a completely different kettle of fish to Rupert, and although he was still only nine to twelve months old, he was a real handful.

As the door from the yard into the office opened, a light fawn coloured, skinny and gangly legged, young dog, hurried into the room, a second later and attached to the other end of the dogs lead, a young woman entered the room. Hugo rushed towards me, and then began to sniff me, all the time his tail frantically wagging. I responded and talked to him in a calm manner, and stroked the back of his head – from then on, he stayed by my side.

My husband, son, and Peggy, then one by one introduced themselves to him, with Hugo, as we later named him, responding in a friendly way.

On the journey home my son Mark, sat in the front seat of the Land Rover next to his dad, who was driving, I sat in the back with the two dogs.

The Land Rover is the old type with bench seats at ether side at the back of the vehicle. Peggy took up her usual seat, in a corner near the back door, and I sat behind the front passenger seat.

Hugo sat next to me, and was so close there was no gap between us; I put my arm around him, in an attempt to reassure him.

What was he thinking, I wondered. I knew Peggy would do her best to reassure him, and I hoped she would let him know he would come to no harm with us.

Hugo behaved perfectly for the first twenty-four hours – then the fun began, or so to speak. He began to show his dominant side, but I very quickly realised that this was a defensive reaction. For him, it was a case of, I don't know you, and I'm not sure what you are going to do, so if I growl a bit you may go away. When he realised I would not allow him to intimidate me, he became very quiet and wary. We don't allow dogs on our sitting room furniture, and its one of the first things a dog learns when coming to live with us. Hugo was used to doing things his way, and got a shock when he made himself comfortable on our sofa, only to find me at the back of it tipping him off! He didn't know what to do, and after giving me a backward glance he left the room. It was obvious to me that this dog did not want to be a tough guy, he was just so afraid of what might happen to him if he allowed anyone to become close to him. He had realised that if he growled people usually backed off, and I can't blame anyone for that, after all a nine to twelve month old Great Dane is already larger than the average adult German Shepherd.

Hugo found it difficult to put his trust in any human, and who could blame him, his life so far, had been full of turmoil and apprehension. It was obvious that he didn't know what was expected of him, regarding relationships, and his place in the family, and society. This, I believe, is through no fault of his own but because of the circumstances he found himself in, from birth onwards.

Over the next few days, and weeks, Hugo showed all kinds of behaviour patterns, which led me to believe, that he had not had sympathetic and constructive guidance, at the beginning of his life as a family pet. Cupboard doors that were opened in his presence caused him to really cower, and shake. We can all only guess at what had happened to him in the past. He was extremely jumpy, and on edge all the time, and never relaxed. When he was let out, into the garden, he didn't know what to do – he just paced up and down within six or seven paces, all the time just going backwards and forwards. It was like when you see those programmes on television about captive wild animals, such as bears, and tigers being kept in extremely small cages, and just being left there, to eventually die of despair. Only, Hugo was in our garden, and not restrained at all let alone in a small place behind bars. The open space just seemed too much for him to cope with. Perhaps life so far, hadn't included exploring new situations, and so Hugo had become wary of everything and everybody who wasn't a part of his normal day to day life – whatever that was.

Peggy keeping watch

Hugo appeared not to trust anybody, or anything, so it wasn't easy getting him to put his trust in me, and my family, and as with many relationships, it would be built up over many weeks, months, and even years.

From the beginning, Hugo hated being left in the house even when Peggy was with him. He did all the usual things associated with this, like chewing things up, only being a Great Dane, the damage was greater. Although he was never left for long periods of time, he still managed to chew and rip off door frames. It was amazing what he was able to do in that short time.

Puppies and young dogs, are renowned for chewing things like the legs on chairs and tables – well this also happened with Hugo only it didn't stop there. The top of the kitchen table was chewed off, and the scratch marks on the back door were like something from a horror film and there was a hole in the door the size of a football (needless to say it was replaced with a more solid one!).

At night, the dogs in our house have always slept in the kitchen and this was no different for Hugo, only when we went upstairs to bed at night, Hugo would begin an unrelenting, very loud howl. This didn't just last for the usual few nights it usually takes for a dog or puppy to settle, it went on continuously for at least the following six weeks. Although this behaviour put a great strain on our family relationship, we were not about to give up on him. Every dog is an individual, and should be treated as such – he needed help, and we wanted to help him. We decided to try and ignore his unacceptable behaviour as much as was possible, and reward him with praise, contact, and treats, for the behaviour we wanted, we found that praise and physical contact were the best reward for this individual, as he wasn't very food orientated, but thrived on gentle human contact and kind words. I felt that the most important thing to do was for us to gain Hugo's trust and confidence.

I kept my distance but also gave him lots of hugs and encouragement – that sounds contradictory, I know, but it's true. I knew Hugo was one of those dogs, with whom you have to be one-step ahead, so to speak, but he was now a member of our household, and we were prepared to work with his behavioural problems, and give him a future.

Whacky races

The one time I wasn't one step ahead of him at the beginning of our relationship, proved to be, for me, quite an experience.

Hugo was hurtling around the garden at great speed one morning, and I was on my way to the shed at the bottom of the garden. A couple of times he went whizzing past me, then on the third, he very softly caught hold of my arm, in his mouth, and there was I, whizzing round the garden with him!

He wouldn't let go, he thought it was a great game. About the second time round, I started lagging behind; I knew I had to do something. Luckily for me, I had on a jacket that was a size or two too big for me (well it was something I only put on in the garden, we've all got one, haven't we?) and Hugo was holding onto the cloth, and not my arm.

Somehow, I managed to wriggle out of it – after stumbling to the floor, loosing a wellie, and a few more turns around the garden that is. I sat there on the ground, as my jacket went flying on in front of me. Eventually Hugo stopped, dropped the jacket on top of me, licked my face, then stood there wagging his tail, as if he were saying, "that was good wasn't it, I really enjoyed it, can we do it again sometime!"

For weeks afterwards, every time I went in the garden with Hugo, I put on something I could easily get out of. Fortunately, it never happened again.

Although Hugo had made friends with Peggy, (I think he saw her in a matriarchal role), he was very wary and defensive on coming into contact with other dogs.

In short, Hugo had very little canine social skill, and even less canine/human relationship skills. This is something that is learned through interaction with littermates, and various people, at a very young age.

For Hugo, most dogs, and people were met with suspicion and defensive behaviour. He just didn't know what was expected of him, or how to react in any set of circumstances. Early general socialisation to my mind is paramount regarding training requirements that I consider the most relevant to the Great Dane.

An adult Great Dane, who has not been adequately socialized is far more difficult to keep under control, and is less acceptable to society, than an adult Yorkshire Terrier, who is lacking in social skills, and who may be allowed to get away with things because of their size.

With frequent walks around our village, Hugo began to learn. On approaching other dogs, if we got too close, he would crouch down and shuffle backwards; when we got past, he would always bark. So I made sure there was enough distance between him and them for Hugo to be able to walk past without too much distress. It's really sad to see a member of such a majestic breed lacking in social confidence. If you're not prepared to let your new puppy become a part of your social life, why get one in the first place.

By now, Hugo and I, had forged a distinctive but trusting relationship, and he accepted my family, although it was with me, whom he sought reassurance and guidance. Looking back at our time together, I see now that I had in fact become very protective of him.

A few months down the line, and when Hugo had confidence in us, and trusted us, I decided it would be a good idea to go to training classes, not that Hugo was difficult to train, because he wasn't. He always responded well to any training we did at home and thoroughly enjoyed it, it was more the social aspect I was interested in, I thought it would help him to gain confidence with other dogs and people. Anyway, we joined a local training club – we were given a place in the beginner's class that lasted six weeks. On our first evening, Hugo and I walked into the hall and we seemed to be the first to arrive, it was a large space surrounded by chairs all around the edge. We were directed to one of the chairs at the bottom end of the hall.

Hugo and I sat there patiently waiting for the rest of the class to arrive. Slowly people and dogs began to arrive, most of the dogs there were young puppies, and of varying breeds. There were representatives from the Akita to the Dachshund, and virtually everything in between.

Hugo behaved well, although a little agitated until a man with a collie dog sat in the seat next door but one to us. Hugo barked frantically; the next thing, the trainer in charge of the class told Hugo and I to go through the door next to us and into the kitchen.

When she came in to see us, she opened the serving hatch that looked out onto the hall containing all the other dogs and their owners. She said that we should stay in there and we were to watch all the other dogs walking around, we were told if Hugo managed that without incident, then we may be able to come out and join in.

Hugo didn't utter a sound although he was visibly excited by what was going on, and I could tell he wanted to join in. About twenty minutes later, we were allowed out!

Looking forward to life together

One of the calmer dogs, with handler, was placed a short distance in front of us and began to walk around the hall, we were to walk around behind them and at the same time keeping that distance. Hugo responded well, he loved it, he was taking part!

The weeks went by, and we joined the rest of the class more and more, although they all still kept a distance of two chairs away from us, Hugo, although still wary of the others, did start to relax a little, and I know he really loved doing the exercises, and we even got to walking around with the rest of the group at a normal distance, and were able to weave around the other dogs and handlers without incident.

He was never going to be totally relaxed, and without social problems of some sort, but believe me this was a breakthrough, and an enormous achievement. At the end of the six weeks there was a presentation and prizes were given to the three dogs who carried out the exercises with the most competence, obviously Hugo was not among those three, but he was awarded with a special rosette with the words *well done* on it, for the enormous achievements he had made, regarding his feeling of fear and uncertainty in the company of other dogs. As you can imagine, that rosette is, and always will be among my most treasured possessions.

I must point out though, that the training classes were never a *cure* but they did help Hugo to cope with life, and they helped me to cope with Hugo. So, during the summer months when our particular class and trainer stopped using the hall and instead took to the local park/playing fields, we felt confident enough to join in – Hugo enjoyed it immensely. In the autumn we rejoined the indoor class, but unfortunately a couple of new members in our next round of classes thought that Hugo distracted their dogs so much, that they didn't learn anything!

When one evening Hugo and I were getting ready to go to classes, and the phone rang, I was shocked to hear the voice of the trainer on the telephone telling me that these people didn't think it was worth their while carrying on if Hugo was there because their dogs found him such a distraction. The trainer said she needed the business and asked us not to attend!

All these years later, I still don't understand?

Washday

Over the next few months, Hugo finally started to settle into some kind of normality – in so far as he stopped chewing things up - although he did start an annoying game – to me anyway– of taking my washing off the line for me.

Hugo found it great fun, as quick as I was hanging the washing on the line, he would grab it between his teeth and pull it off. It was no good not letting him out until I had propped the line up as high as it would go either, because in that case he would take a running jump at it, and dog, clothes, and pegs would fly through the air at great speed, landing in a pile on the ground, to which Hugo then thought it good fun to roll in his chosen article of clothing, and needless to say the washing process had to begin all over again!

Despite Hugo's love of washday, by now it was clear that he realised that this was his home, and that we were his family – I think for the first time in his life so far, he felt secure, and a part of something.

***

Unfortunately, turmoil was just around the corner.

It was a lovely day in late summer; Hugo was enjoying himself in the garden, when I heard him cry out. As I looked out, I saw Hugo suddenly drop to the ground. I ran out of the back door, and into the garden, Hugo was still laying on the ground. My eyes met his – they were full of pain and asking for help.

After hugging, comforting, and reassuring Hugo, he slowly began to stand. I could see what a great effort this was for him – Hugo couldn't stand to full height, it was as if there was something stopping him, pushing him down.

My first thought was that he had injured his back in some way. He had been running around the garden, at great speed, I thought, maybe he had turned too quickly, and pulled something. I told him, I would get some help for him, and make it better.

On telephoning the vet, I was asked if I could get him to the surgery because that was the best place to diagnose, and treat him. I agreed to meet the vet there. It was a Sunday, so my husband was at home, he helped with getting Hugo onto the back seat of the car, and then I also got into the back of the car. Hugo was lying with his head in my lap, and Alan was driving. It's just a short journey to the vet, ten to fifteen minutes, but that day it seemed to take an hour.

Hugo had visited the vet before for inoculations and he was also castrated – I can't say that it made any difference to his behaviour though – and because of his mistrust of humans, had worn a muzzle on those occasions.

Although he seemed very subdued, I didn't want to take any chances, so took the muzzle along this time as well. I was confident that he wouldn't show any aggression towards me, but what about the vet.

On arrival, Alan and I very carefully helped Hugo out of the car. When we got inside, I told the vet of Hugo's history, and we decided to put the muzzle on him whilst he was being examined. I felt rotten really, making him wear this thing when he was unwell, but I knew it was as much for his protection, as it was for the vet. He could have very easily interpreted his pain, as being the vets fault.

He was very good throughout the examination, and not once did he show any sign of aggression. Anyway, the vet suggested a possible spinal injury, and thought it best to hospitalise him overnight, with the intention of taking some x-rays in the morning.

It was horrible leaving Hugo there. What did he think? Did he think we had abandoned him?

Around mid-morning the next day, I received a telephone call from the vet. I was told the x-rays had been done and a spinal specialist had been consulted. The x-rays had shown a small bubble like form, attached to Hugo's spine, at a point somewhere between, his shoulders, and neck.

The specialist thought that it was likely to be a tumour, and had gone on to suggest taking Hugo to a canine cancer specialist. I couldn't believe what I was hearing – my Hugo couldn't have cancer could he?

It felt as though my heart had jumped into my mouth – my whole body was hot and tingly, and I experienced a feeling of dread, emptiness, and unreality all at once.

I wanted to be with Hugo for the journey, so knowing that Alan was working many miles away on that particular day, I contacted my brother-in-law, who was self-employed, to ask for help. He very kindly agreed to take us on that sixty mile journey.

The cancer specialist was contacted and about half an hour later, Hugo and I were once again travelling together in the back of a car. We were shown to the waiting room when we got to the hospital. Hugo seemed to me, to be a little better, he was certainly standing and holding his body in a more natural position – was he recovering, or was it just the drugs that he had been given? A couple of minutes later, a vet came into the room, he introduced himself, and said that although he had been given information from my vet, he would also like to hear my version of events. I told him what had happened the day before, and filled him in with Hugo's background. The vet then took Hugo away from us to undertake more tests. Hugo was very quiet now due to the effects of the drugs he had been given. About half an hour later, we were called into a consulting room, where the vet was standing with Hugo. I was given a definite diagnosis for Hugo of spinal cancer. The vet showed Tony – my brother-in-law – and I, the x-rays – and yes, there was definitely a bubble on Hugo's spine. I was then asked if I had any medical insurance for Hugo, I remember what a feeling of relief it was for me to be able to say yes.

From there I was informed that Hugo needed to spend some time with them at the animal hospital, and another test would be done, and then possible chemotherapy treatment.

The vet advised me that all this could cost in the region of £4,000 and was I sure that the insurance would cover it. 'Yes it would'.

I hugged Hugo and tried to reassure him that things would be all right, and that I wasn't leaving him, I would definitely be coming back for him; all I was doing was trying to make him better. Did he understand? I then reluctantly left Hugo, in what I thought were capable and sympathetic hands.

The journey home was silent.

I telephoned the hospital the next day and was told that Hugo was undergoing more tests, and that someone would call me the following day. I wanted to know how he was, but the nurse said she had just come on duty, and didn't sound like she wanted to be helpful. I think the attitude of the nurse should have alerted me to something, and under normal circumstances it would have, but I wasn't thinking straight at the moment, with everything going on – I just wanted Hugo home.

The next day, that phone call came. The cancer specialist informed me that, although Hugo was walking a lot better, he thought that was just the effects of the drugs, and that his chances of survival were very slim.

He went on to suggest that I either had Hugo put to sleep, or come and pick him up, and think about it over the weekend, he also said that he didn't expect Hugo to survive more than another seven days or so.

I was shocked. I couldn't see how he had deteriorated so much, so quickly, but I knew I had to bring Hugo home. Arrangements were made for us to pick Hugo up, I told the vet we probably wouldn't arrive there until after six p.m. because it was now very late afternoon, and we had to travel a good distance, also there would be a lot of traffic on the road at this time of day.

It was early that same evening that Alan, and I arrived at the animal hospital.

At reception we were met by a very unsympathetic and abrupt veterinary nurse, who told us that no animals were discharged this late in the day. I explained we were expected, and that we had travelled quite a distance to get there. The nurse mumbled something about how late it was – it was about 6.15 p.m. – and disappeared, I supposed, to find a vet.

I was relieved to see the vet who had examined Hugo on our arrival three days ago, enter the room. He went on to tell us that fortunately he lived on site, or as the nurse said, we couldn't have seen anyone.

I answered by saying that 'he knew we were coming, it had been arranged earlier in the day, between me and himself, and I had also said we would possibly arrive after six p.m. due to the distance of our journey'.

The vet then said we would have to wait – for what I don't know. I asked if I could see Hugo while we waited, and after a discussion between the nurse and vet, about how we should pay the bill first, we were directed to a room at the back where Hugo was being kept. All I can say is that I was and still am appalled at the conditions they were keeping Hugo in. My poor lad was in a pen with some wet and soiled bedding, and an empty water dish – he looked as though he was giving up. I quickly took Hugo out of the pen; he was very lethargic, and disorientated. His character didn't come through at all, he seemed totally crushed. He was also damp, due to his soiled bedding.

As I was hugging him, and telling him, it would be all right now, and we had come to take him home, I heard a booming voice behind me, 'what on earth do you think you are doing,' said the voice.

I aired my opinion on their level of care, and to that I was told that I couldn't take Hugo off the premises until I had paid the bill in full. All I wanted to do was get Hugo out of there, and fortunately, I was able to pay up. With hindsight, and having grown older, and I hope wiser, I should have refused, and asked for the police to be called (not everyone had mobile phones then). You see, we were unable to just walk out of the building, due to a security lock; a member of staff had to let you out. On my first visit, I had thought this to be a good idea, well I didn't want someone going in and stealing Hugo. Now, it seems this lock has a number of uses.

Hugo clung to my side and I kept a comforting hand on him all the time. It felt very oppressive in that building just then and I think the three of us had a feeling of relief as we went out into the fresh air.

Alan picked Hugo up, and put him gently down in the back of the Land Rover, and I got in after him, vowing never to take an animal there again.

I just held Hugo, as I have already said he was in a very subdued state, it was as if my Hugo was not inside this body, as I held him, I knew he now felt safe, and after all he was in his Land Rover, his safe place.

When we reached home, the first thing Hugo did was to go into the garden, and relieve himself, he looked pathetic as he took a wobbly walk around, checking if everything was still the same.

It must have been extremely traumatic for him, hanging on, regarding his water and bowel movements until it was no longer possible.

Whatever else Hugo did, he was always clean, and from the moment he had joined us, I had never known him to have an *accident*, so that made the conditions he had been kept in at the hospital all the more appalling.

Hugo smelled like a public lav, and I knew he felt uncomfortable, so after giving him a drink, I got a bowl of warm water, a sponge, and some baby shampoo. I just gently washed him down, in the hope it would make him feel more comfortable, he didn't need urine burns on top of everything else, did he.

Once he was cleaned up we all went inside. Hugo and Peggy greeted each other, Hugo then went to his bed, and slept for hours.

How was I going to make this up to him?

Over the next few days, Hugo began to improve. He settled back into his daily routine, and gradually looked healthier, and stronger.

I certainly wasn't going to take him back anyway, but I did decide to take him back to our local vet to get him checked over. So a few days after Hugo seemed to be settled again, off we went. The vet was amazed at the improvement in Hugo. He was standing, and walking in a normal manner, and was happy. I remember thinking, surely this can't go on. Here was a dog, who had literally been given only a few days to live, and now here we were over two weeks later, and he was running around as if nothing had happened.

If Hugo ever did have cancer, a miracle must have happened, because from then on, he just went from strength to strength.

There is no way that I can explain the *bubble* on Hugo's spine – and it definitely was there, I saw it on the x-rays, and so did a number of other people. But, whether it was, or wasn't cancer, I don't think he would have made any progress if he had stayed at that particular animal hospital.

The fruits of autumn

One day in early autumn, I heard the usual vocal tones of one of our neighbours.

'Are you there lass?' – not that I'm a lass anymore.

It was an old gentleman in his eighties, who was a retired farmer, and still kept himself very active. He had an orchard, and small piece of land, that ran alongside our garden, where he grew a number of fruits, and vegetables.

I walked round from the back garden to the side, and there he was, 'Oh, you're there lass', 'do you want some plums?' I said yes please and thank you very much. My neighbour then handed over a large bowl of lovely ripe plums.

Hugo, Peggy, and I took the plums into the kitchen. I took a few plums out of the bowl and placed them on the drainer, by the sink, intending to wash and eat them. The telephone rang in the next room, so I went to answer it. When the conversation had finished, I went back into the kitchen, but where were my plums?

I looked in the sink, thinking they may have fallen from the drainer into there. No, they weren't there, I looked around the room, they were nowhere to be seen. At that moment, Hugo came to my side. He sat down in front of me, and looked straight at me. It was then that I noticed his cheeks, they were bulging and lumpy, I opened his mouth, and there were my plums! I put my fingers in, and took them out. One-two-three-four-five! Each plum was still perfect, with not one puncture, scratch, or graze to be seen, they were all still perfectly formed, and not at all squashed.

To me that showed how gentle Hugo could be.

Summer holiday

Seeing as we now trusted Hugo not to chew the house up if we left him with Peggy for a few hours, and most importantly, he trusted us, we decided to book a holiday, in Wales. There is never any question about the dogs coming too, so with this in mind, we looked for accommodation, most suitable for the dogs.

We found a lovely little cottage down a country lane and also close to the sea. They took dogs, but having large dogs, I only think it fair to reveal their breed when booking. If you don't, it could come as a shock to the owner of the accommodation on your arrival. Well, let's face it, most people's idea of family pets are dogs like terrier, or Labrador-size. Having done all this, the time arrived for us to embark on our journey.

At that time, we travelled around with the dogs, in the same Land Rover that we had taken Hugo home in from the rescue kennels, and from that awful animal health place and he seemed to have developed a fondness for it. He must have felt safe when he was in it, and had a feeling that things could only get better from then on, he always sat in the same spot as well. I saw this as a bad thing really, and I certainly didn't want Hugo to become defensive of it. Training had begun to defuse this, before it got out of hand, but we still had work to do.

We made a few stops on the way, so that dogs and humans could stretch their legs and relieve themselves, and of course, Peggy and Hugo were sometimes left in the Land Rover on their own for a few minutes. It was at one of these times when we had parked up so that we could use the public toilets on the other side of the road.

As I came out of the toilet, I noticed two young men were walking down the street, on the same side of the road as the Land Rover. One of them noticed Hugo sitting in the Land Rover – anyone who has a big dog will know that they can attract a lot of attention from people you don't know. Anyway, the two young men approached the Land Rover to get a better look. Hugo was standing up by this time and was watching them. He waited until they were very close to the window, and then out came his booming bark. As you can imagine, the two men jumped back, looked at each other, giggled, then carried on walking.

Hugo didn't stop though; he carried on barking, and jumping about in the back of the Land Rover. I could hardly believe what I saw next. The Land Rover just moved slightly from side to side, in a zigzag kind of way.

It just goes to show the importance of early socialisation and training, especially when the dog in question is so large. I don't think Hugo would have harmed those men; on the contrary, I think he would have cowered down and backed away from them – they had already walked away when he started jumping about – but it could have really frightened someone, or another dog.

We made another stop before reaching our destination, and this time, I provided some light entertainment for my son and stepson.

I got out of the Land Rover and attached Hugo's lead to his collar. I then led him to a grassy patch by the side of the road in order for him to relieve himself.

Hugo was excited about getting out for a while, and tried to take off at great speed – with me attached to the other end of the lead!

Needless to say I went flying; well, in fact, I fell straight down, face first, just like a falling tree!

Hugo, by this time, had remembered about me, and turned round to see what had happened.

He began sniffing me, and then licked my arm, which was grazed rather badly, all the time his tail wagging enthusiastically. I could almost hear him saying, 'what happened to you', 'how did you get down there?'

My fall also caused great amusement for my son and stepson too, who were falling about, not because of an accident, but with laughter!

And even today, all those years later, it's usually brought up without fail, in conversation, at family gatherings, by one, or both of them!

***

Time passed, and Hugo matured. Although the situation had greatly improved regarding Hugo's socialisation, it was clear that there were always going to be some situations that Hugo would find difficult to cope with. I accepted this, and just tried to give him the support he needed, as, and when it was appropriate.

Life for Hugo, was at last, fairly normal, until that is, a few months later.

Both dogs, and Alan, were outside, in the garden. Alan came inside, and said, there was something wrong with Hugo. I rushed outside, and was confronted with a really pitiful sight. Hugo was standing hunched up, and retching. Right away, I suspected stomach torsion, (though I had never come across it before, I had read up on it, because Great Danes are among the breeds susceptible to it). We went to the vet straight away.

The vet confirmed my suspicion, and asked permission to operate. I signed the consent form, and went home, to wait by the telephone, for hopefully some good news.

A number of hours later, that telephone call arrived. The operation had been a success, and Hugo was recovering. The vet and I then discussed what was going to happen next.

Usually after this type of operation, the nursing and after care, is done by the veterinary nurses, and the dog is hospitalised for a number of days.

Because Hugo was such a big dog, and quite nervous, the vet suggested that they would keep him for the first night, to make sure he had no adverse reaction to the operation, and then, I was to nurse him at home.

Although I knew it was going to be really hard work, really I was glad that he was coming home the next day; you see I missed him so much.

Hugo was going to need lots of rest, and care, in a quiet environment. With this in mind, we cleared the dining room of furniture, so that he would have plenty of room to lie down, and move properly, and that became 'Hugo's Hospital'.

It's quite a shock when you go and collect your dog after such a major operation. Hugo was still looking just as pitiful has he had done the day before, and this time he had a great long line of staples stopping his insides from falling out. He was also, understandably very subdued.

It never ceases to amaze me – the amount of trust and love a dog will show you, even when they themselves are very poorly. Despite all this, Hugo managed to gently wag his tail when greeting me. I really appreciated this gesture; I put my arms around him, and very gently hugged him.

The vet gave me instructions on what I was to do.

I was to check and clean the wound – and believe me it was a big wound, and shocked me – administer antibiotics, and painkillers, start him off on a very small light diet of chicken and rice, building up to a normal diet, and take him out into the garden with his lead on, to relieve himself. He wasn't allowed to run free for six weeks in case the staples burst. That brought with it the need to clip Hugo's nails; you see, he wasn't getting his usual walks out and about, on pavements and such, so they now had to be clipped. I felt a bit nervous about this at first, I was frightened of clipping too much off and making it sore, well that's the last thing he needed right now. Fortunately, all went well.

It didn't stop there; I felt it would aid Hugo's recovery, if he knew how much he meant to me. The only way I could do this was by spending quality time with him. Of course, it took time to administer medical care, but I believe in cases like this, it boosts the recovery process to show the dog, or any animal for that matter, just how much you care. I spent many hours hugging Hugo, talking to him, and just being there for him.

Through that time, I think my relationship with Hugo grew stronger, and we became even closer. I cared for Hugo over many weeks, each time we visited the vet for a check up, he was stronger and stronger. The vet was very pleased with our progress and eventually life got back to normal, and we all began to enjoy life again.

Just over one year later, Hugo suffered another stomach torsion, it was hard to believe, and taking precautions to try to stop this from happening was part of our everyday life. It was nothing unusual for us, living with Great Danes it just becomes part of your normal daily routine.

The vet said this torsion wasn't as severe as the last one, although the same procedures would have to be followed. The wheels were set in motion, and Hugo recovered very well again.

I feel that I can't stress enough, how rare it is for a dog of any breed to survive two stomach torsions. The chances of surviving one are slim. All I can put Hugo's survival down to is the speed in which he was seen by a veterinary surgeon, at the onset of the condition.

Stomach torsion

I have no veterinary training, but I will do my best to explain, from experience, and compare how I saw what was happening to Hugo, with what is written in various veterinary and canine health guides.

This is a condition that could affect any dog with a deep chest, but isn't thought to be hereditary. It is an acute condition with a high fatality rate even for dogs that receive immediate veterinary attention. A dog of any age should never be fed for at least one hour before, and after exercise. The reason for this is that dogs with large chests can become bloated (swollen, or inflated, due to gas in the stomach) if exercised shortly before of after a meal. When this happens it could develop into stomach torsion (the stomach twists). This prevents food from entering or leaving the stomach.

The outward signs are swelling of the abdomen, drooling, and retching. Hugo didn't drool, but he did retch nor did he restlessly wander – he just stood still, with what looked like an arched back – and a very swollen stomach, become listless, or show signs of pain, (the fact that Hugo was so quiet and still lead me to believe he was in pain), symptoms of shock quickly develop. Hugo was definitely showing signs of shock, and his eyes were asking us for help.

Most dogs will show the same or similar symptoms as stated in the veterinary and canine health books, but you must also remember that just like people, dogs are individuals, with individual ways of coping with things.

Even though all the precautions are taken, this dreadful thing can still happen, as Hugo and I found out, not once, but twice.

I can't stress enough the need to act quickly, and get veterinary help. To see your dog in so much trouble is heart-breaking, even when they have recovered, and in our case, all these years later, my mind still holds that dreadful picture of suffering.

Even though you know that you have done everything in your power to stop this from happening, you still think, there must be something else you can do – there isn't.

The next couple of years with Hugo, although restricted in some ways, were very pleasant. He seemed to realise himself that he was a little different regarding sociability, but my relationship with him couldn't have been any stronger – perhaps under other circumstances it might have been.

We just seemed to click, and totally understood each other.

The fact that Hugo completely trusted me was a very special thing, considering, at the start of his life, he had been so terribly let down by his human companions, and I feel extremely privileged that he chose me as the person he would actually trust with his life.

Over the months that followed, our relationship grew, and Hugo blossomed into a handsome adult Great Dane.

On a personal note, I took great pleasure from watching Hugo play. At first when he came to us, he didn't know how to, and certainly didn't have the confidence to follow it through. So I saw this as a great achievement, there is nothing as rewarding as the first time an emotionally-damaged dog of any age, actually has the confidence, and feels so at ease in your company, that they pick up a toy, and play with it, just like a young puppy would. And that reward becomes much greater when that special dog is no longer afraid to interact with the people and other dogs in the household by means of play.

It was now late summer 2000; it had been a pleasant summer, and Hugo was spending most of his time relaxing in the garden.

As soon as I went downstairs in the mornings, he would greet me in the kitchen, and then immediately ask to go outside; yes he did want to relieve himself, but more than anything he wanted to go out, and stay out, in the warm sunshine. He loved the warmth of the sun on his body as he lay on the lush grass.

I often sat looking out of the window, with a cup of tea in my hand, just watching, as he lay there, calm, and unafraid.

By this time, Peggy, our Lab cross, (who was I think, a mother figure to a number of rescue dogs brought into our home), was approaching her eighteenth year. So it was nice that both dogs had reached this sedate stage of their lives together.

As I sat watching the dogs, I remember thinking, how nicely things had settled down, and I felt happy, knowing that Hugo was finally enjoying his life. Although he didn't, and never would, trust other people and dogs entirely, he did cautiously tolerate them. All these achievements made life much easier for all of us. With this in mind, I felt relaxed and content, he was greying now, but life had become calm for him at last.

Just a few days later, our lives changed for the worse.

Hugo had always been a fussy eater, or should I say choosey, and I always thought he should eat more than he did. It was always challenging to get him to eat what I thought was the right amount, and throughout his life with us, he, in my opinion, had always been a little on the slim side. But surprisingly, recently, he had been eating enthusiastically.

Well for a couple of days, during this particular week, he had been off his food just picking at it really, nothing would tempt him. Then he started to bring up bile, and was obviously feeling unwell. So without hesitation, I took him to see the vet.

Off we went in *Hugo's Land Rover*. Alan was driving, and I sat in the back with Hugo, telling him not to worry, the vet would make him feel better very soon.

However, that was not to be. Hugo was diagnosed with kidney failure, which could possibly be caused by an infection. A blood sample was taken in the hope of finding out the extent of the damage, and he was also given a steroid injection. We were sent home with glucose to put in his water.

This was a Friday, and over the weekend, Hugo picked up, became more alert, and even ate some steamed chicken and rice. I was elated, and thought, *yes, he is going to get better*: well Hugo always did – didn't he. He always managed to give just that little bit more.

As arranged I telephoned the vet, on the following Tuesday, to find out how Hugo was doing, and to give me the results of the blood test.

I didn't want to say out loud what was happening now – that would make it true, wouldn't it.

Things had changed again since the weekend, and I was feeling unsure and subdued as I told the vet what had happened. I now thought – no that's wrong, I now knew that Hugo was going down hill again.

The vet said that it must just have been the steroids that had made Hugo feel better for a short time, and that the blood test had revealed that a very large percentage of Hugo's kidney was not working. This was devastating news, the vet went on to say that all we could do was see how he coped with it. The kidneys had probably been deteriorating since birth. How could this happen, how could he have become so dangerously ill, so quickly. This time last week, everything had appeared normal, with Hugo relaxing in the garden, just as he should be. I lightly-cooked some chicken and rice, enough to last Hugo a few days; it would keep in the fridge.

I offered food to him a few times a day; I was prepared to feed him a little at a time by hand – if only he would take it; He just wasn't interested.

I hugged and kissed him, all the time talking to him, in a calm voice, hoping to reassure him, to make him feel loved.

He tried so hard; he really wanted to live.

Late on Saturday night, Hugo was asleep in his bed. He was so tired, but so determined to carry on. I caressed him, and spoke gently to him. I was trying to reassure him by staying calm, but if the truth be told, inside I was crying and felt despair.

The next morning Hugo was still in his bed, thankfully, he had been sleeping. As I walked towards him, he gently wagged the end of his tail, he tried to stand up, but couldn't. I went to lay down with him, caressing him, as I had done so often throughout his life.

He told me it was time; and I agreed.

After telephoning the vet, and arranging to meet her at the surgery, Alan picked up Hugo, and lay him on the back seat of the car, (during the past few days, Hugo had lost so much weight, if I hadn't seen it, I wouldn't have believed it possible), I got in , and sat with Hugo's head resting in my lap. I gently stroked his head throughout the short journey.

As the car approached the surgery, the vet came out to meet us.

We decided that the best place for Hugo to be as we helped him on his way was to leave him right where he was.

He was slipping into unconsciousness. I didn't see the needle go in: I kept my eyes on his face. His image was becoming blurred through the tears that I could no longer hold back. It didn't take long, just a few seconds: Hugo went limp, and his face relaxed.

I didn't want this. My heart was breaking – had I done the right thing? The vet asked what we wanted to do. Did we want to leave Hugo with her, or did we have other arrangements.

I didn't need to think about it, he was coming home with me.

As we journeyed home, I held onto Hugo, his body now moving with the motion of the car: I held him.

The car stopped outside our house, Alan got out, and then opened the back door for me to get out.

I said 'no, just leave us for a while.' Hugo and I spent a little more time together before I got out.

I had to. Alan and I had accepted the role of godparents for one of our nephews and today was the church service.

As much as I just wanted to stay at home, and grieve for Hugo, I knew I couldn't let people down, on such an important occasion.

So, I reluctantly left Hugo, in order to get on with the life that was carrying on around us.

We have a fairly-large garden that already accommodated the graves of previous pets, so it just seemed right that Hugo joined them. Alan dug the grave in a large flowerbed, and as you can imagine, it had to be of a substantial size to accommodate the body of an adult Great Dane.

We lay Hugo on his blanket, and gave him his favourite toy, which I hope he is able to play with as much as he wants to now.

Alan and my son, Mark, gently lowered Hugo into the ground – I went back inside the house.

For many weeks after, I couldn't help thinking, there must have been something I could have done differently, and should I have consented to euthanasia?

Of course, now, so many years later, I know there was nothing I could have done, and euthanasia was the right course of action to take – I couldn't let him suffer.

In my opinion, Hugo was a victim of bad breeding practices.
I have never seen a copy of his pedigree, so have no idea at all regarding his lineage.

My personal thoughts are as ever – that dogs should be bred primarily with good health and wellbeing in mind and not to keep up with current fashion such as to how flat you can get a dog's muzzle, before it stops breathing all together. I know that's not relevant to the way a Great Dane usually looks, but I think it is a good example of how people can become misguided in an effort to create so called canine perfection.

It is really heart-breaking when you know your dog is suffering because of inherited health problems. Surely it would do more to secure the future of any breed, if prospective owners knew that their chosen breed was attributed to good health.

I know there has to be some kind of breed standard, but surely some system could be worked out, to hold in high esteem those dogs belonging to a kennel with a good track record regarding hereditary health issues.

Bentley

On to a lighter note now with Bentley – my Mr. B. He's such a lovely boy.

Bentley came to live with us a few months after Hugo had so sadly left us, and these two dogs are as different as chalk and cheese, as the saying goes.

It all started with a lovely lady who is involved in Great Dane rescue. She knew all about our sad loss of Hugo, and knew that at some time I would want to provide a home for another Great Dane. Bentley was not in the care of the Great Dane Rescue – no, his breeder had *run him on*, i.e. kept him on to show – and had been very successful with Bentley in the show ring, winning both Best Puppy in Breed, and Best of Breed overall, amongst many other trophies by the age of nine months.

Anyway, for some reason unknown to us, Bentley had decided that the life of a show dog was not for him, and had gone from winning all those trophies and rosettes, to not wanting to enter the ring, and not standing properly when asked, well generally just not wanting any part of the show dog world. So, his then owner, being a professional and considerate breeder, decided to retire him from the show world, and try to re-home him as a pet.

What's this got to do with the lady involved in Great Dane rescue you ask? Well, she is also a professional Great Dane breeder, and as such also shows her dogs, and had got to know Bentley's breeder through the dog show circuit.

She had seen Bentley at shows, and had admired him. Then noticing that Bentley no longer attended, she enquired as to his whereabouts. She was then told of Bentley's aversion to dog shows, and that there was a search going on to find him a new home.
She very kindly immediately suggested me!

Telephone numbers were exchanged and contact made.

Over the next few weeks there were numerous telephone calls, and many hours chatting time spent between me and Bentley's breeder. The reason for this was to try to find out what kind of people we are, and the kind of household we live in, so as to make a decision on which home would be best suited for Bentley. As far as I am aware there were two other households who were being considered as potential new families for Bentley, they were as far apart as Scotland, Kent, and us, in Lancashire.

Eventually, Pam asked if she could bring Bentley and his mother Paige to visit us. I was over the moon, but still a little nervous, as I knew that even though they were travelling from Lincolnshire, to Lancashire to meet us, it certainly did not mean that Bentley would automatically be left in our care.

Mid-October, and the morning of the visit arrived. I was like somebody waiting to take their driving test, or get their exam results. I couldn't relax; I was nervous but so excited at the same time.

I heard the car draw up outside – well, I was watching from the window really – and went out to the gate to greet them. A small lady got out of the car, followed by a brindle Great Dane bitch, then a young fawn dog – Bentley.

I couldn't believe how handsome he was – he was everything I had hoped for, and he was perfect.

At that time he was sixteen months old, and a lovely rich fawn colour with a black mask – black markings around the muzzle, and eyes – he also had dark ears. He was perfectly-proportioned, and just beginning to lose his fluffy puppy fur; in fact, that made him look as if he had freckles.

We all entered the house by the front door, and I was handed Bentley's lead. Peggy, our cross bred came into the room, she was now eighteen years old and couldn't care less who came into the house, just so long as they were friendly. She introduced herself to the two Great Danes, who began to relax at once.

Peggy made friends easily, and I know she understood that the dogs who were left in our care, were in need of a secure and loving new home. Peggy kept a watchful eye on all of us, and always knew when, and how, to give her support.

At our first meeting, I sensed that Bentley was a reserved character; in fact, quite shy in some ways. Even though he had been in many dog show situations, he was not accustomed to everyday life and experiences associated with family life in general. By that, I mean things like family member's comings and goings, general household machines, e.g. the sound of washing machines and vacuum cleaners and such like.

I understood that all this was new to Bentley as was, our family. But I knew we were going to get on, and that when he had learned to trust us, he would take most other things in his stride.

After spending a few hours with us, Bentley's breeder, and his mum, Paige, headed back to their home, leaving Bentley in our care.

Bentley seemed to look to Peggy for comfort, and she responded in her usual caring, motherly way. She gave him a warm welcome, and I'm sure she told him that he had nothing to fear from us, and that everything would be all right.

Bentley's first night with us passed without incident; he, and Peggy, settled down together, in their soft warm bed and had a good night's sleep.

Next morning, when I went downstairs and into the kitchen, a lovely, warm feeling washed over me as both dogs got up out of their beds, and walked towards me, to greet me, and say good morning. Although Bentley had been living in kennels for most of his life so far, with intervals of living in a house for a few days at a time, there was no problem with house training – he never had one accident.

Later that day, I decided to take Bentley out for a walk – show him around his new village.

Anyone who has ever had a canine companion knows how much pleasure a dog can get out of just a simple thing like going for a walk. So, when I picked up Bentley's lead, I wasn't expecting his reaction at all. He walked away from me and tried to hide – not easy for a Great Dane! He wasn't shaking or anything like that, and he certainly didn't show any signs of being frightened of the lead. It was strange – he just didn't want to have his lead clipped to his collar.

Because I knew his background, I was quickly able to understand what was happening. Nothing bad or aggressive had happened with the lead; it was just simply that Bentley associated having his lead clipped on with being taken to dog shows.

For the next few days, I picked up the lead within Bentley's view, at intervals, and clipped it to his collar for a few seconds at a time. Once the lead was on, he just accepted it, and never showed any sign of dislike. It must have purely been the thought of going to a dog show. It only took about a week for Bentley to realise that I was not going to take him to a dog show. It was really good then because, he then started to get excited on production of his lead, and was eager to go out for a walk, even though he was wary of some aspects of his new environment. You see, up to being sixteen months old, Bentley had lived in largely what was a kennel environment, and was only taken away from his home environment to be taken to dog shows, so he was unaware of, and sometimes fearful of some everyday scenarios, and objects in the outside world.

He really did enjoy going for his walk, but was fearful of some buildings, temporary signs that appeared, some traffic noise, and sometimes even things blowing about in the wind.

I felt really sorry for Bentley; although he was happy and content, I knew he would enjoy life much more if he was able to overcome these fears. I tried to help him – Bentley and I spent many hours in each other's company, supporting and encouraging each other to overcome these fears, and to get more from life.

Regarding his fear of some buildings, I knew it was no good just avoiding them, because we could be confronted with something similar, wherever we went, and I wanted Bentley to enjoy a full and active life.

As we approached these buildings, Bentley's whole body would tense, and this feeling would travel through Bentley and up the lead to me. I tried hard not to tense up myself, because I wanted him to be able to feel how relaxed I was, in the hope that would help him to realise there was nothing to be afraid of.

As we reached a point, a few yards away from the building, Bentley would make his fur stand on end, in an attempt to make himself look bigger than he already was. He would then sit down and refuse to move forward.

I asked myself what it was about the particular buildings that he didn't like, but just drew a blank. They were all different in style, size ages, and even colour. One was a brand new red-bricked building, and another 300 year old cottage painted white.

We didn't avoid these buildings, but I also didn't want Bentley to get anymore stressed than he already was. So every day, we took a different route that would incorporate one or more of these buildings. We approached the buildings, walking on the same side of the road as them. Then at a point that I sensed was just before Bentley would react, we crossed the road, and carried on the same route, but on the opposite side of the road to the building.

Bentley, of course, was still aware that the building was there, but instead of stopping dead, and refusing to move forward, he carried on walking past the building, but at a distance. For a number of times, at first, Bentley's fur stood on end, but he did carry on walking, without stopping. As we walked on, I constantly told him what a good boy he was, and how brave he was too, I also stroked his shoulders gently as we walked in an effort to reassure him – that's something you can't do with a small dog! I was so pleased that he had enough confidence in me to keep him safe, and that he trusted me enough so soon in our relationship to feel that I would not lead him into danger, this carried on for another three to four weeks, then when Bentley finally stopped doing his impression of a pom-pom as we walked past on the opposite side of the road I decided it was time to try to pass on the same side as the buildings.

That afternoon, we walked through the village, and down the road towards one of the dreaded buildings. As we walked, I talked to

Bentley, in a calm and clear manner. I told him what a good boy he was, and how much we all loved him.

We carried on down the road; the building was now in sight, so-far so- good. I felt apprehensive for Bentley, but tried to think of something else, because I didn't want to relay that feeling to him.

As we reached the point where Bentley would normally react, I looked straight ahead, to a point passed the building – that's where we wanted to be.

As we carried on, Bentley's pace ever so slightly quickened, then his fur fluffed out; but he carried on, he didn't stop. He was such a brave boy. With me at his side, he walked passed the building.
A few more weeks on, and Bentley was able to walk past all the buildings at a leisurely pace, and without fluffing up, head held high with confidence.

What a wonderful feeling it is, when you know a dog trusts you enough, to conquer his fears.

During all this we were also building confidence regarding sights and sounds. This was achieved by sitting in strategic places around the village, to enable Bentley to get used to world he lived in without causing him too much distress.

Fortunately for us, there is a grassed area, with a bench on it, at one end of the road we live on, and there are always cars travelling up and down a road just to the side of the grassed area. This was ideal for me and Bentley. We would go and have a sit down and a chat for ten to fifteen minutes each day – weather permitting. My idea with this was to help Bentley to realise that traffic noise is just part of everyday life, and to take it in his stride. By doing this, Bentley also became accustomed to things blowing about in the wind, and everyday life and changes.

I tried to ignore the panicky fearful behaviour, as much as possible, and praised and encouraged him through his achievements.

All these were gradual achievements that happened over a number of weeks and months. As with any dog, but especially dogs that have been re-homed, for whatever reason, you must always remember that they have no idea at all, who you are, or why they have left their previous home. All they know is that they are suddenly in a new environment, with people and maybe other dogs and animals they have never met before. All you can do is give them love, understanding, and patience, and that will give you the basis of a lifelong relationship.

Anyway, as Bentley's confidence in us grew, so did his character. By Christmas, he had been with us for a couple of months, and he was now definitely a valued family member.

On his first Christmas morning with us, there was as usual, presents under the tree with Peggy's name on them, and of course, this year, among them was presents for Bentley. Peggy was used to this and always knew which her presents were – she also needed no help to unwrap them! I have many cherished memories of Peggy, but something that always springs to mind is the way she frantically unwrapped her presents on Christmas morning – tail wagging, and excitement in her eyes.

This Christmas morning, I called Bentley to me and showed him which presents were his. He was interested in the ones with treats in them, and even helped to unwrap them by clawing at them with his paw. With my help, he revealed his chocolate bones, and other such doggy delicacies. He also had an oversized tennis ball, he didn't seem to play with toys much, but when he did it was a pleasure to watch. I rolled the ball along the floor and at first, Bentley just watched it, but with a bit of encouragement – that means me going after the ball on all fours to show him what to do – he got the hang of it. Well, kind of. He would go after the ball and pick it up, and then lie down and hold it in his mouth for a few seconds. I could see we would have to work on this.

Christmas dinner was successful, with the dogs as usual having their turkey dinner just like us. This was the first time I saw my Mr. B dance. Well, that's what I say he did. He watched as I put turkey, sausage, sprouts, carrots, gravy e.g. into his bowl, and I could sense his anticipation. As I gave it to him he took his first mouthful, then started padding all four paws on the floor alternately, it looked as if he was doing a little dance of joy; I suppose really it was an interpretation of the thing tiny puppies do when suckling from their mother. They kind of gently pad at the flesh surrounding their mother's nipple when having their milk. I think it's probably either an attempt to make the milk come quicker, or a sheer pleasure response, or why can't it be both.

Anyway, I know Bentley was getting a lot of pleasure from his Christmas dinner.

'Lassie moments'

By the spring of the following year, Bentley had mapped out a familiar daily routine for himself, and as on most bright, sunny mornings, he and Peggy were in our back garden together, exploring the flowerbeds, and the hedge.

As I watched from the kitchen window, I saw Bentley sniffing at the plants directly around the pond. Due to the pond's close proximity to the kitchen, most of the plants in that area are herbs; they are very pungent to us humans, so to a dog, with their fantastic sense of smell, herbs must be very alluring. Bentley carried on his investigation for the next few minutes, seemingly unaware of my observation. Then he very quickly jumped back ever so slightly, as if he had caught sight of something from the corner of his eye. His head moved in short sharp movements, and his tail wagged gently. I realised then, that his eyes were following the movement of the fish in the pond.

As anyone who keeps fish, in an outdoor pond knows, the fish are fairly dormant through the colder months of winter, and tend to stay towards the bottom of the pond, and barely feed.

As soon as the water has been warmed up by the heat of the sun, the fish become more active, coming to the surface of the water, and searching for food. This is exactly what was happening in our garden. It was then that he felt my presence, as I watched him from the window. Bentley then came through the open back doors, and into the house. I thought *Oh, I've spoiled it now, I've distracted him, and he won't do it again*. Well, I was wrong.

Bentley came into the kitchen, and stood directly in front of me. He began lifting his paws up and down, as if walking on the spot. We made eye contact, and his eyes were switching from me, towards the direction of the doors, and back again to me, as if he was indicating that I should go to the door. That wasn't all though, he started to pad back and forth – to the door, then to me – back and forth. His mouth was slightly open and he was making a kind of faint squeaking sound of enjoyment and excitement that dogs seem to do. He was definitely asking me to follow him – now you know the reason for the heading!

What else could I do? I asked him to show me, and followed him outside.

Once at the pond, he looked at the fish swimming in the pond, and then gently nudged me with his nose, and indicated with his eyes for me to look in the pond. This happened a few times, from fish – to me- then back to fish again. I did what he asked and looked at the fish. It was as if he was saying to me, *look what I've found, hurry up, come and look*!

I said *yes, they are fish, aren't they nice, you are a good boy aren't you?* He seemed so pleased with himself, and he wanted to show me what he had found.

I knew Bentley had very good canine social skills, but this proved to me what I already really knew – that he was very good at communicating with humans, surely that must be a sign of intelligence in an individual dog. Not all animals can deal with cross species communication in such an easy manner. I understood straight away what he was saying to me.

Since then, I have caught him on a number of occasions just quietly watching the fish, and when he senses me there, he looks at me with his laughing eyes, and gently wags his tail, as if in recognition of what we share.

I wonder if watching fish is as therapeutic for dogs, as it's supposed to be for humans.

A similar thing happened a year or so after that. As usual, in good weather, the back door leading onto the enclosed garden was open, so that the dogs could come in and out as they pleased. I was also in the garden, enjoying being with the dogs and all of us taking advantage of the warm weather.

Bentley came rushing down the garden to me, from where he had been busy, near the back door. He had that look of excitement in his eyes, and his mouth was partly open, as if he was grinning. Again he was eagerly indicating to me that he wanted me to follow him. "Come on then," I said, "what have you found?"

Bentley posing in the garden

On reaching the point at the top of the garden where Bentley had been, he took me to a paving slab that had been left lying against the fence that divides the back garden from the side garden. Anyway

Bentley did that thing with his eyes. You know, he looked at me, and then, to-and-fro, from me to the paving slab. He wanted me to look down at the other side of the slab.

I took a step forward, Bentley at my side, tail wagging, and his mouth slightly open - still smiling. I could hardly believe what I saw then. Just laying there between the slab, and the fence, was a little brown fury animal. I think it was a stoat. It looked a bit like a ferret, but was a lot smaller.

I looked at Bentley, and told him what a good boy he was, and thank you, for showing this to me. *What a lovely dog he is*, I thought to myself.

Although I knew that Bentley would not hurt the little animal, I also knew that the animal would not move from that place, while we were around. After all, it had no way of knowing that we didn't want to eat it, did it? So, we went inside for a biscuit, and a drink, hoping that would give the little animal a chance to move on.

A little later, Bentley and I went outside again. Bentley went straight to the stone slab. I followed on behind, and then took a look down the side of the slab. I said to Bentley, "Look it's gone," and pointed to the ground. Bentley, looked down and sniffed the ground, he also very gently touched the ground where the stoat had been with the whiskers on his chin. When he had finished, Bentley, turned round to look me in the eye, he then licked my nose, (his way of giving a kiss), I said, "Thank you, Bentley," and he moved off into the garden to investigate some more.

There were many of these *lassie moments* over the coming years, from things like, Bentley finding hedgehogs, to interest shown in pottery figures of dogs. Each one is a very special cherished moment for me.

Time moves on

As anyone who has given a home to a *second-hand* dog knows, that depending on the background, and personality of the particular dog, it can take many months, and in some cases, even years, for a dog to totally settle into a new home.

With Christmas over, and the winter rapidly turning into spring, Peggy and Bentley's relationship had developed, and they had become great friends. As always Peggy was looking after Bentley, making sure he was settling in well.

By May of that year, Bentley had been with us for about seven months, and had got used to our everyday life. Peggy was now around eighteen years old, and had seen my son, now twenty-two years old, through his childhood and into adult life. My son, and Peggy, had many happy days together, over many years. Peggy had been a play mate to him, in the garden, and around the village, she had been there to see us all through good and not so good times, and was a greatly loved, and important family member.

Peggy's latest task, of course was to ease Bentley's transition into our family.

Peggy was always there for us, and always listened to what you had to say, she also knew exactly how to comfort you if you were feeling down, as we all do from time to time.

She was now well into her old age, and had survived two small strokes, fortunately without any debilitating after effects, and although she had arthritis associated with old age, was still able to lead an independent, and as far as her age would allow her, a mobile life style. She was also a sufferer of *selective deafness*!

We, of course, tried to make her life as comfortable, and as enjoyable as possible.

She was definitely enjoying her old age, and although I knew she was on *borrowed time* – being in her eighteenth year – it didn't stop me from feeling shocked when, on-going downstairs one May morning, she was lying in her bed, in obvious distress.

My heart dropped down to my feet.

I went to Peggy's side in an attempt to comfort her and find out what was wrong.

We made eye contact and I knew straightaway she was in serious trouble. She didn't want to move, and I knew she felt really ill, and was probably in pain, although she never made a sound. I do think that sometimes, in cases of severe pain, it causes animals and people to be quiet, rather than express their distress vocally.

I immediately called the vet, who asked if I could get Peggy to the surgery as she may need treatment that would be better carried out there.

My husband said he would drive us there so that I could comfort Peggy. I sat in the back of the car with her on my lap.

Throughout her life, Peggy had always become excited at the prospect of a car journey, and amazingly, although she was so ill, she wanted to sit up and look out of the window, she even gave her tail a little wag.

It never ceases to amaze me, the way dogs, even when faced with serious problems, are always able to see the good side of life.

On reaching the surgery, we were taken straight into a treatment room. The vet examined Peggy, but the expression on her face told me everything, even before she spoke, I knew that this was as bad as it could be.

Peggy was diagnosed with internal bleeding. It was explained that it was probably a benign tumour in her stomach that had ruptured.

There was no alternative than to put her to sleep.

I couldn't think straight, *how could it be? Isn't there anything else we could have done?*

70

I hugged Peggy, and told her that I loved her, she looked at me, and I knew she was saying the same. Then she felt limp, lying in my arms, and I knew she was gone.

On the way home in the car, I held Peggy in my arms, she just looked like she was asleep.

Of course, she got her special place in the garden along with the others she had known. I know she had a long and happy life, but that doesn't stop this feeling of devastation at her loss, and a hollow empty feeling inside, not quite believing what has happened.

But now, I had to cope with the fact that as in any multi-dog household, the surviving dog(s) may need help coping with their grief.

The day Peggy left us, Bentley began to act differently, and he just didn't know what to do without her. To begin with, he just didn't settle as easily as usual, and he was on edge. Then when I gave him his dinner that evening, he picked at it, like a child playing with their food. It was as if he was waiting for something, he did eventually eat it, but it took quite some time.

The next day I could tell Bentley was feeling down, maybe even depressed. Anyway, he mopped about, not really interested in anything, and didn't want to do anything.

I tried to explain to him what had happened and that Peggy would not be coming back. Well, if you think about it, how confusing, not to mention frightening, it must be for a dog to know their canine companion has been taken out of the house and driven away never to be seen again. Imagine that happening to people, and not being given an explanation for it – it's got to be just the same for dogs. I'm sure they must wonder if the same thing is going to happen to them.

I tried to reassure Bentley, telling him he was a good boy, and how much I loved him. I made a point of spending more time with him than I already did.

He was as always keen to go for a walk, but now, once out, he hung his head down, that wasn't normal for him, he usually walked along, head held high, as proud as could be.

I knew he was missing Peggy, so was I; but what else could I do? I couldn't bring her back.

By the end of the first week without Peggy, Bentley had become quite depressed. I can hear some people saying, *Oh, don't be daft, dogs don't get depressed.* Well, I know that they do.

I believe that dogs have feelings, thoughts, and intelligence. So any living thing possessing these surely is capable of emotion, and depression.

I believe that Bentley understood I was trying to help him, but couldn't yet control his emotion regarding the loss of Peggy.
Peggy had been a kind of foster mother to him, so it stands to reason, that he would mourn her death.

I feel that I must explain that although so far I have known a number of different dogs, with different personalities, as with all of them, I haven't known another quite like Bentley.

You see he has a very loving and caring personality. He genuinely cares about the other dogs and people around him. In his eyes, you can see sympathy, understanding, and tolerance. He gives hugs by gently placing his head on your shoulder, and staying there for a number of minutes at a time, but if you are upset, he will stay there for as long as you need him to, so I know his reaction to the loss of Peggy, is one of genuine grief. I tried to console him, but it didn't stop him from going off his food, and at the start of week two, he was barely eating anything.

Over the next two to three weeks, Bentley gradually began to join in with the family again, although he was obviously still grieving. It seemed that a dark cloud hung over everything that he did, and of course by now, he had lost quite a bit of weight.

I was very worried for him, and decided that Peggy had left such a large hole in all our lives, that although you can never replace a dog who has died, you can provide a loving home for another one.

I thought that this would be the best thing that I could do for Bentley, in this particular situation. He had always been in the company of other dogs, first at the kennels where he was born, and later, here with Peggy, so I thought it may help him to have another canine companion.

As I have said earlier, Peggy had been a member of a litter of puppies handed over to the RSPCA for re-homing, and because she had given us so much joy, companionship, and love over so many years, we decided to look at our local RSPCA re-homing centres in the hope of finding our new companion.

We decided as Bentley was a dog, we would look for a bitch, but hadn't really got any preferences as to breed type or size, but we did want a fairly young dog. Bentley was approaching his second birthday, and we wanted them to be able to play together.

After looking in the two local centres, we decided on a little female dog, who was approximately ten to twelve months old, white with black spots and of the English Bull Terrier type, probably crossed with a collie.

I was told that Mariah, the name given to her in kennels, had been picked up as a stray in the nearby town. Residents in a particular area had contacted the centre after the dog had been scavenging through rubbish bins for a few days. She had now spent about eight or nine weeks in kennels because whenever people came looking around the centre in search of a new dog, she always made a lot of noise barking at them, and she put people off – but not me!

This behaviour wasn't a true representation of her character. Really, she was very friendly towards people and loved a cuddle. Unfortunately, many dogs end up without a home, because of this behaviour that some of them seem to show whilst in kennels.

Something just clicked between us, so after finding out her story from the staff, we decided she was the one for us.

It was agreed that we would bring Bentley to visit this little dog, to see how they got on with each other.

Visit day

Together with my husband and Bentley, I travelled to the re-homing centre on a bright sunny morning in June. On arrival, and after kennel staff had made a fuss of Bentley, we were shown into a paddock. We sat down on a bench seat placed about halfway down the enclosed area. Two of the kennel staff brought Mariah in. *I'll have to change her name*, I thought.

Bentley and Mariah greeted each other, and extensively sniffed every inch of each other's bodies, and then suddenly they turned and began running around the paddock side by side, each making sure the other didn't get left behind. We and the kennel staff all giggled in delight, it was obvious that the two dogs would be friends for life.

A short while later I called Bentley to me, he came running towards me with a smile on his face, and delight in his eyes, I said to him "Do you like her?" He communicated to me that he did, and then it came to me that we should call her Milly. After going back inside to fill in the relevant forms, we went home to wait for an RSPCA home checker to contact us. A few days later, and with the check completed Bentley and I arrived at the centre to collect Milly, and embarked on our lives together. Over the next few months, the friendship between Bentley and Milly blossomed. They became inseparable. They cuddled up together at night, and even shared food. Watching them play was a joy. Of course, Milly was – well I was going to say – more agile than Bentley, but I think that's the wrong word for such a big dog, and he is big, measuring thirty-five inches to the shoulder. Bentley was able to turn very quickly and did everything that Milly did, all be it a little slower, so I'll just say, Milly's sharp turns were sharper than Bentley's.

They played together like any young dogs do, you know, that play fighting they do, but no-one gets hurt, I think that kind of play is very important for young canines, because it teaches them how far they can go, before someone gets hurt, and hurting the other dog, or getting hurt themselves is something they definitely don't want to happen.

You would think that with such a great difference in size, between Milly and Bentley, there would inevitably be accidents and someone would get hurt – but no, both of them are very conscious of each other, and of themselves.

Milly

They ran together, Bentley making sure he didn't leave Milly behind, and you can imagine the amount of ground a Great Dane can cover in comparison to a little terrier in the same amount of time.

None of us would ever forget Peggy, but it made me really happy to see that Bentley and Milly had become such great friends. It was time to move on and I know Peggy would not have wanted it any other way.

Bentley was once again enjoying life – and eating up all his meals.

Unfortunately though, the eating up of meals was short-lived. Just in a matter of a couple of weeks after Milly had arrived in our home, she started her first season. After being a stray and staying in the RSPCA kennels for a number of months, she must have relaxed when she realised she had got a home, and that triggered her body into starting her first season. I had already made arrangements to have her spayed but of course this had to be postponed now.

Bentley, being an entire young male, became very interested in her. I had to split them up – Bentley carried on living in the kitchen where he had always been, and Milly went to live in the dining room for a few weeks – previously Hugo's Hospital.

It's not as easy as it sounds though; well, when you think about, anything dog-related, you now have to do twice. Instead of feeding them both together, it now became one, and then the other. I didn't, of course, take Milly for a walk during this time but had to leave her in on her own when I went out with Bentley. At these times, she would give me that look of *What have I done? Why can't I come too?* Letting them out into the garden had to be done separately too, and instead of in general spending time with both of them together as we went through our daily lives, I had to make a point of going into the dining room to spend time with Milly, after all I couldn't just shut her in there and abandon her. That was all very time consuming, but the worst part of all this was when Bentley stopped eating again.

It can be very distressing living with a dog who has problems due to their sexuality. During the weeks that followed, and although I kept the two dogs apart, Bentley became very distressed in everyday life. He was no longer interested in food, and whatever I offered him, he refused. He was offered a whole chicken, beefsteak, anything at all that may tempt him – nothing did. Bentley also began to howl at night, if you have ever heard this sound, you will know how lonely and haunting that sound is. I asked my vet for advice, and was told not to worry as long as he was drinking enough water as he would not let himself starve. Although I knew this, Bentley's health was on my mind constantly, I can't stress enough how distressing this was for the whole family, even when he started to eat again, it was months before he gained the weight back.

At first, he began eating just a little, which was like an enormous breakthrough; his appetite had to be built up gradually. It took about another two weeks for Bentley to eat normally again, but it was about another four to five months, before Bentley regained his weight totally.

Milly, of course, was oblivious to all this concern, and a couple of months later, when her body had matured and returned to normal she was spayed. Now both dogs live happily together, and I know this problem won't occur between them again.

With things back to normal, life carried on. Bentley and Milly had enjoyable holidays with us, both at the seaside and in the countryside, the sea air, or a warm summer breeze in the countryside enjoyed by us all. The relationship between dogs and humans was growing all the time.

We spent many enjoyable and memorable hours together, either on holiday, out for walks, or just relaxing or playing in the garden.

Red rosette day

Mid-July in our village was a time of great activity for the farming, and the wider community. It's when the annual Agricultural Show is held.

Previously, there had been a dog show-taking place there, but this had been left out of the proceedings for the past few years, but probably because it had been greatly missed, this year. 2003, was the year it was to return.

I had made the decision to go on day two of the show, in order, like most doggy enthusiasts, to look at the dogs. It was a bright sunny day, but not too hot, and the show ground is just across the road to the back of our house, so we are able to come and go to the show as we please.

Bentley enjoyed social outings, made all the better for meeting other dogs, so I decided to take him with me, anyway I could easily bring him home if he got fed-up.

That afternoon I brushed him as I always did before an outing - like us, dogs want to look their best when out for the day, clipped his lead on, and off we went.

It was really busy – there were thousands of people there. We made our way to the dog show enclosure, on the way we met my husband who had been on the show ground since this morning, and all three of us went to the dogs!

I was a bit concerned as to how Bentley would react in a dog show environment, given his history – but I needn't have worried, he was so relaxed and laid back, he wasn't bothered at all.

At the ringside, we watched and Bentley lay down disinterested, as the serious pedigree classes took place – this would once have been the kind of classes that Bentley would be entered into. After a short break, the 'novelty' classes were to be held, there were things such as waggiest tail, best trick, best rescue and most handsome dog at the show. My husband suggested we enter Bentley for that – given our dog's past, I wasn't sure. I didn't want to upset him in any way, or spoil his day, but he was relaxed, and he did trust us completely. I gave it some more thought, and I agreed to enter him. My husband was going to take Bentley into the ring, and I was going to watch at a point where

Bentley could clearly see me. I also told my husband to withdraw immediately if Bentley felt at all uncomfortable.

Well, what a delight – Bentley trotted in to the ring by Alan's side, and then stood there in position, as proud as punch, with an expression of delight on his face – Bentley I mean, not Alan! You can guess what happened next – Bentley was given the first place rosette. We gave him hugs and told him what a good boy he was, along with the rosette, he also won a small bag of food, which we took home, and gave him for his tea.

I already knew how handsome Bentley was, and didn't need a rosette to prove it, but even so, it is one of my most treasured possessions, and is kept in a box with all the other rosettes Bentley had won before he came to live with us, and which Pam very kindly gave to us.

***

In September 2003, I decided to enrol Bentley and me in a Canine Studies course at our local agricultural collage, this involved taking a dog to every lesson.

For myself, I wanted to increase my knowledge, and enhance my relationships, regarding our canine friends.

For Bentley, I hoped it would be a source of great enjoyment, and act as a confidence boost.

So, at the start of the academic year, Bentley and I set out to take our places in collage.

Bentley enjoyed meeting new dogs and people, although he was sometimes quite shy with people, you couldn't fault his canine social skills. I wanted him to get more from life than he already did, he did lead quite a full life compared to some Great Danes, and I know he was always happy and content, but sometimes he did stop himself from doing things that he really wanted to do because of his shyness. I suppose it was something like a shy child who looks on at other children playing games and would love to join in themselves but they can't, because their shyness stops them from doing so, and they end up just standing and watching, as others enjoy themselves. I thought that maybe this course, with my help, could help him in some way.

Well, I know I couldn't expect Bentley to overcome this completely, but I thought that the fact that he and I were doing things together, away from a familiar environment, would make it easier for both of us to join in group activities together – we would be supporting each other.

Bentley loved to make new friends and it was obvious that he thoroughly enjoyed joining in with class activities. As well as all the academic work done throughout the year, there was a training program undertaken during the summer months. This was when the whole class was able to get outside for part of the lesson, and have some fun.

I could sense Bentley's excitement as we stood in line waiting our turn to do the exercises we had been given, and hopefully at the end of this, Bentley would get a certificate of his own, that being Federation of Dog Trainers and Canine Behaviourists, Companion Dog Awards. There is gold, silver, and bronze awards – we opted to do the bronze. It would mean practicing at home too, and a source of more enjoyment for us. Our tasks included such things as a kind of relay dog obstacle course, for which we were put in teams, food refusal, walking to heel, control of dog off lead, and many other enjoyable tasks.

The fact that I could potentially get a City & Guilds Level 2 qualification and other federation awards took second place as long as Bentley got his, which would please me most.

Bentley was four and a half years old now, and in Great Dane terms, that means he was middle-aged. I've always felt it very unfair that a dog like the Great Dane, who can be such a fantastic canine companion, should only have an average life span of eight years. In the summer of 2004, when the course ended, Bentley had already started showing signs of ageing. He had begun to show signs of mild arthritic change in his left back leg, and that lovely black mask on his face was greying. I was able to help him out with the arthritis by making sure he ate healthy and fresh food, and the vet prescribed some anti-inflammatory/pain-killing capsules that were made from natural products. Within a week, I noticed a big difference – it was obvious Bentley was feeling more comfortable. From now on, it would just be a case of managing the arthritis, which certainly didn't seem to stop him from enjoying life as he carried on as normal. We did all the things we had always done, but, of course, in moderation, and in a sympathetic manner, according to the situation at any given time.

We completed the course and Bentley got his certificate – it made me very proud – and I got a distinction!

Things that go beep in the night

I was really pleased with my shiny new microwave oven. I unpacked it and set it up in the kitchen, whilst all the time talking to Bentley and Milly. As usual both dogs responded by actually looking interested in what I was saying and vigorously wagging their tails. They listened whilst I told them about the new microwave and how it also worked as a grill and convection oven – we really would have to learn how to use it properly over the coming weeks.

A number of weeks had passed, when at around two a.m., I was woken to low sounding short bursts of barking. It was Bentley; this was very unusual, he very rarely barks, and when he does you know there is a good reason for it. My first thoughts were that there must be somebody creeping around outside – or if Bentley had been caught short and needed to go outside. He doesn't usually do this, but anything could happen, couldn't it?

Alan was sleeping soundly besides me – it would take more than that to wake him! I got out of bed and went downstairs to investigate, all the time listening trying to hear any noise that there may be if someone was outside, but everything was quiet: By now, Bentley had stopped barking, and I could hear him moving about at the other side of the door that leads to the kitchen. He was aware that I had responded to him, and was waiting to greet me. The house was quiet, but as I turned the handle of the kitchen door I could hear a beeping noise – I opened the door into the kitchen, patting Bentley as I went in. I looked to the direction from which the noise was coming from. From there, I could see that the digital timing display on the microwave was showing end – which means end of that particular cooking time – and the beeping noise is the sound that alerts you to that event. Also, the beeping happens once every minute from then until you take your food or drink from the oven. I opened the door of the microwave, there was nothing inside, but it stopped the beeping. Bentley didn't appear to be bothered by anything now so I put his barking down to the beeping annoying him, after all I wasn't sure how long it had been going on for, or maybe there had been someone or something outside, but there wasn't now, and when I asked Bentley if he wanted to go out he immediately got back in his bed, so it wasn't that either.

My explanation was that possibly my son, who was in his early twenties at the time, felt hungry when he had returned home after an evening out and somehow had not operated the microwave correctly. Anyway, Bentley was settled and tucked up in his bed, and Milly had shown no concern for anything so I went back to bed and thought no more of it. That is until a couple of days later when I got up at around seven thirty a.m. as normal and went downstairs into the kitchen. There it was again – that beeping sound coming from the microwave. Bentley and Milly got out of their beds and came to greet me – they didn't seem at all concerned about the beeping noise, although it would annoy most people if that noise was going on and they couldn't do anything to stop it. I opened the door of the microwave and closed it again to stop the beeping. When my son came downstairs, I asked him if he had used the microwave the night before and possibly not turned it off properly. He said he hadn't used it at all in the past few days, and there our conversation ended as he dashed out of the house to get to work. I didn't know what to think.

That night it happened again, just the same as before with Bentley uncharacteristically barking and me going downstairs to put things right.

Was it the beeping that was bothering him, or was there someone lurking about outside? It could it be a fox, or some other small animal. I went back to bed and gave it some thought. My explanation of Bentley barking because the beeping annoyed him after a while was feasible. Or was it just coincidence that the two things happened at the same time and really he was barking to alert me to something. There had been a number of break-ins and robberies in the area lately – was it connected to that? But then Milly kept quiet during all these occurrences which for her was unusual, because she is one of those dogs who has too much to say for herself, and freely offers her opinion! I saw her being quiet as a good sign because if there was someone lurking about outside, Milly would most definitely let us know. But even if there was someone there it wouldn't explain the apparently self-starting microwave would it? It crossed my mind that maybe it was a ghost, but why would it want to use the microwave for goodness sake! Then I felt silly for having thought that and went back to sleep.

The next morning I asked my husband if he had used the microwave the night before – he was on my list of suspects along with my son – but he also denied my accusations. I was determined to find the culprit.

A couple of weeks passed and although Bentley had stopped barking during the night, the microwave hadn't stopped beeping, so, either he had got used to the sound and it didn't bother him anymore, or he had been barking for some other reason.

On quite a number of mornings now I had gone down to the kitchen and been met with the beeping sound of the microwave. I was sure it was either my son or my husband – one of them I thought, just wasn't doing something quite right when using the thing.

A few days later whilst relaxing in the sitting room with a cup of tea and a magazine, my relaxation was interrupted by a sort of whirring sound: It was coming from the kitchen, and it sounded like the noise the turntable makes as it goes round in the microwave, so off I went into the kitchen to investigate. The light was on inside the microwave and the turntable was indeed going round. Who had done this? There was only me and the dogs, who, by the way, were having their afternoon snooze at this moment in time. It couldn't be my son or my husband they were both out at work. Was it some kind of fault, or was it truly a ghost?

By this time, I was becoming quite concerned. Everybody says you shouldn't run a microwave with nothing in it, yet here was mine seemingly pleasing itself when it would run. Over the next few days, it happened frequently, sometimes three or four times a day, and on one occasion, I was actually in the same room; I had my back to the microwave, making a cup of tea, and chatting to the dogs telling them we would go out for a walk when I had finished my tea, when suddenly I heard the microwave start up – I turned round, and there it was, light on, turntable going round, and three minutes left on the cooking time! That was scary, I can tell you. I didn't have the tea, but picked up the dogs' leads and went straight out for our walk. Whilst out, I calmed myself down and tried to think of an explanation. Was there a fault with the microwave, or was it something more sinister, and what could I do about any of it?

Friends and family decided that we must have a ghost and for some reason it was trying to make contact via the microwave. I could understand why they thought that, although it seems silly I had wondered myself but preferred not to think about it. I thought the best thing to do would be to contact the manufactures as it could be something that happens all the time – even if it didn't, they may have an explanation.

I telephoned the relevant customer service department and mentioned about the microwave turning itself on at all times of the day and night. "It even does it when I'm in the same room, can you help me please?"

The lady taking my call sounded shocked and said she had never heard that before. "My goodness," she said, "I'm glad that hasn't happened to me, I would have run out of the house screaming." She then very seriously asked me if I had a ghost. I was surprised at her reaction. I know the same thought had crossed my mind but you don't expect *helpline* people to say things like that do you.

The outcome was that arrangements were made for a carrier to pick up my microwave and take it back to the manufacturers who would then carry out tests in an attempt to find out what was going on. They also said that if they found the fault to be of my making I would have to pay the transit, investigation, and repair costs. I was happy to go along with this as I was confident I was not to blame.

Three weeks later, I was happy to receive a brand new microwave from the manufacturers. I unpacked it, but unfortunately there was a large dint in one side of the oven. Also, I had expected a letter of explanation as to why my original microwave supposedly had a mind of its own, so I telephoned the number I had now been given for assistance. The company representative apologised for the damaged microwave and suggested it may have happened in transit, because it would not have been allowed to leave them in that condition as everything is checked before leaving their warehouse. Arrangements were made for the oven to be picked up from my house, and I was told that once the company was satisfied that my actions could not have caused the damage, a new one would be despatched to me.

I then asked what the problem had been with the original microwave oven; the gentleman had a look through my file but said it seemed quite strange, but he couldn't find any details regarding the tests, and he wasn't sure if he could access that information anyway. *Oh well*, I thought, *perhaps a letter would arrive separately, explaining what the problem was*. I did want to know though, because you don't know if microwaves are causing any damage do you when they don't work properly. A week later, another new shiny microwave arrived at my door. This time everything was fine, but there was still no explanation regarding the original oven. I thought *Well, I've got a nice new microwave, do I really need to know what was wrong with the other one?* The answer to my question was that yes I did. I called customer services again to make enquiries and this person too said exactly the same thing as the last one – there didn't seem to be any details on the tests, or the cause of the problem, just that authorisation had been given to send a new one to me. I still wanted to know, but left it at that for now anyway, thinking, I'll give them a couple more weeks, and then write a letter to them asking for an explanation.

My new microwave took its place on the kitchen worktop and was up and running. The next few days passed without incident and I was pleased with my new machine. Then one morning when I had got up and gone downstairs into the kitchen, there it was again – that beeping sound coming from my new microwave! My first thoughts were *What am I going to do now, I can't send a third one back, can I?*
Over the next few days, the activity intensified – usually when I was out of the room. As soon as I heard a whirring sound – and I had started to listen for it – I would go into the kitchen, and there it would be, light on, turntable going round, and then BEEP as it stopped. I couldn't understand what on earth was going on?

It didn't seem to bother Bentley, or Milly – well why should it? They've had plenty of time to get used to it now, haven't they?

"What's going on?" I said to them. *They must know, they live in the kitchen don't they*. Bentley and Milly responded with that look most dogs have, you know, those wide-open eyes, with that look of understanding, and gestures of sympathy. *They would tell me if they could*, I was sure of it.

I started to believe what people were saying to me about it being a ghost trying to contact me for some reason. So, I decided to switch off the microwave at the mains and pull the plug out when it wasn't in use – and thankfully that stopped it!

The nose in question!

A couple of months passed. Most of the time I did remember to pull the plug out with a few exceptions though.

Then, on this particular afternoon, Bentley, Milly, and I had enjoyed a good walk, then on returning home we all went into the kitchen. The dogs settled down, and I started to prepare the vegetables for our evening meal. I turned round to talk to the dogs, and that's when I saw him! No, not a ghost, but Bentley, and no, he wasn't switching the microwave on, but he WAS pressing the buttons on the washing machine, with his nose. There he was, pushing the buttons on the washing machine, then standing back and waiting for a reaction. It put me in mind of those laboratory experiments scientists carry out using all kind of animals to test their awareness and intelligence. You know the ones where they get them to press something or choose a specific course in order to be given a reward. *Was Bentley pressing things to find a response, and that response was his reward? He certainly has always been very inquisitive and very self-aware. Was he finding out about the world around him? Was he the phantom microwave operator?*

I needed to find out, so decided not to pull the plug out anymore but try and catch him in action. It didn't take long. The next day as I walked into the kitchen from another room, there he was. I kept quiet and didn't move. Bentley stood facing the microwave for a few seconds, moved closer to it, then – I could hardly believe what I was seeing – he put his nose close to the panel that housed the operating buttons and pushed the settings button a couple of times, following by the pushing of the start button – and hey presto, the microwave started up! Bentley watched for a few seconds, then went and made himself comfortable in his bed. I went into the kitchen and said to Bentley, "so it's you then?" and yes I got that 'Who me?' look

Could it be possible Bentley had learned that the beep of the microwave would probably bring me into the kitchen? Talk about response to a stimulant, was Bentley training me?

That's when I remembered all the trouble the microwave manufacturers had gone to in replacing my oven. *I've left them in the dark so to speak and I do feel a little guilty and a little silly but I can't tell them, can I?*

By now, Bentley was showing signs of the ageing process. That lovely black mask covering his face was greying, and although his arthritis was apparent, it was well under control using the natural products from the vet and a good fresh diet. In the main, Bentley showed very little symptoms regarding his arthritis and coped with it very well indeed, so it never was a real concern. I also think that changing Bentley's diet from processed dog food, to one inspired by the BARF diet has helped all my dogs to live a happy, healthy life.

Bentley was now six years old, and I had decided it would be nice to have a younger Great Dane around too. My idea being that the everyday things Bentley did would rub off onto the younger one, and eventually I would have two Great Danes with a calm and easy-going nature. You see, Bentley took most things in his stride, and for me, had become the perfect housedog. I didn't want to lose this, so my decision to become a three-dog household was made. I already knew that the breeder – Pam – who had brought Bentley to us, was planning a litter of puppies to be born early that summer, so I contacted her, and she was happy for one of the forthcoming puppies to come to us. Although we had previously had dogs of both sexes in our household, we had only ever had male Great Danes, and had it in mind for that to carry on. The breeder kept me up to date with the pregnancy so I wasn't surprised when she telephoned a couple of weeks before the puppies were due. We had a long chat about the forthcoming births, dogs in general, and of course, Bentley, Milly, and all of Pam's other dogs.

A little later that day the phone rang again. It was Pam. *I like to think we get on well and if we needed to we could ask each other for help*, so when she tentatively said she wanted to ask me something, I said, "Well go on, get on with it," wondering what on earth could it be? Pam told me of a good friend of hers, who is also a Great Dane breeder. Her friend had spoken to her that morning and had been upset about a puppy, which she had sold as a pet earlier in the year. Over the past few weeks, the family who owned the puppy had done the right thing in contacting the breeder to ask for help as their circumstances had changed dramatically and they realised they could no longer care for the dog as they felt they should. So, the search for a new home for the puppy was on. Unfortunately, it hadn't been going too well, and all concerned were getting upset. I lived about an hour to one-and-a-half hours away from the puppy, so was asked if I would go and have a look – and perhaps I may become interested in her. I was told the puppy was very lively and boisterous, and needed someone who could devote a lot of time to her, she also had an undershot jaw, which, when I saw her, I realised was in fact overshot meaning her top jaw protruded out over the bottom one. It seemed everyone involved was becoming quite desperate for this situation to be resolved.

I thought, *Well I've never had a Great Dane bitch before, is it what I want?* I'd nothing against having one, I'd just never thought about it, and of course she would have to be spayed, Bentley was entire, and I certainly didn't want any accidents. After talking it over with my husband, I decided the best idea would be to go and have a look. More telephone conversations followed and finally I contacted the family concerned. After a long discussion, I realised it just wasn't the right time for the family to commit to a very large, very lively, demanding puppy, and because of their current circumstances, it would be best all round for the puppy to be re-homed. I arranged a meeting at the family home at the end of the week. Meanwhile, I received some photographs of the young Great Dane by e-mail. My mind was made up as soon as I saw them. She looked so sweet – well we all know what it's like when we see puppies don't we, we can't help but want to take them home! The morning of the visit arrived and I couldn't get there quick enough. Alan was driving and I was trying to make sure we didn't get lost. Amazingly, we didn't – and we arrived on time!

As we parked the car outside the house, the front door was opened by a young woman. *She must have been watching out for our arrival,* I thought. I knew that giving up her dog wasn't going to be at all easy for her, and I have respect for the hard decision she made to actually go through with it. It's very difficult, and very emotional, but to identify that you need to re-home your dog for its benefit, and to actually go through with it before things start to slide and it becomes a real problem is admirable. This way things can be worked out for the dog(s) and people concerned and difficult situations avoided.

After initial greetings, we were shown through the house and into the kitchen. From there the young dog was brought in from the garden, and a big smile spread across my face. The little dog came to greet us – I couldn't take my eyes off her. She was six months old – and so cute. We accepted a cup of tea, and were shown into the sitting room along with the dog, who immediately came to sit by my side and snuggled up to me. The young couple brought in the tea and we all settled down for a chat. I told them about Bentley and Milly, and showed them some photographs of the two of them, discussed the other Great Danes that had been in our lives, and talked of their situation. During our conversation, I found out that no basic training had been done, and the dog, who was called Milly by the way, was not used to being on a lead and was unaware of the world outside her home. I would have to think of a new name for her, and quick, I wondered how confusing this was going to be, and how soon the new dog would realise she was no longer Milly, but my old Milly was still called Milly!

The time had come to go home. Although I so much wanted to take this dog home with me, and felt excited about it, I also felt upset for the young woman giving her up; I know what you're thinking – that I'm just a soft touch. The young woman came to the door with us and watched as the dog shied away from getting into the car – she just wasn't used to this. I sensed the woman was crying, and turned round in time to see her going back inside the house. Because the dog was only six months old, so still quite small, Alan was able to pick her up, and gently place her down onto the rugs and blankets I had put there for her in the back of the car. I got into the back of the car too, in order to try to comfort her. I tried to imagine how she was feeling and what she was thinking. I feel I cannot adequately put into words how much I want to make such a transition as easy as possible for any dog coming into my care, and hope that other people feel the same way. I put my arm around her and talked to her in a kind and gentle manner. I really did hope that she would know that I would never hurt her, and that all I wanted to do was to make her happy. She didn't move all the way home. That is, apart from putting her head in my lap for comfort. It was then I decided to call her Daisy.

Getting Daisy out of the car was nowhere near as difficult as getting her in. I clipped her lead onto her collar whilst her head was still in my lap. Then, as I got out of the car holding onto the end of the lead, I encouraged her to follow me using a gentle coaxing voice. Although she was slightly hesitant, she did follow me. Suddenly, she lunged forward and made for the bottom of the large hedge that surrounds our property. That was it – Daisy just lay there with her body as flat to the ground as she could possibly get it, and refused to move. She laid there with her body stiff and tense, her big eyes staring at me; she must have been really frightened of the outside world. I knew I would have to get her going under her own steam somehow. There's no way that I, or many other people for that matter, could go around picking up a Great Dane, never mind that I wanted Daisy to realise there was nothing to be frightened of. These things were happening because Daisy was not used to being on a lead or being taken out of her home environment, so she had no idea what to expect or how to react. All the new sights, sounds, and smells didn't resemble anything that she had been used to. She had been outside in a garden but that had been a safe enclosed space to her. Being outside in the big wide world just overwhelmed her. In these situations, you have to be sympathetic towards the dog, and don't try to push or force anything. Let them decide when they are ready to move on, and try to support them, not add to their fears by shouting or pulling and pushing. A little gentle coaxing goes a long way, and it provides a stepping-stone for confidence. I wanted Daisy to trust me, and I knew that would take time, weeks, months maybe. Right now, I needed her to find a little self-confidence through me. On first impression, I thought that she liked me, or is that the wrong word? Should I say, she saw me as an authority figure, and accepted that if I lead, she would probably follow. I passed the lead to Alan, and started walking in the direction of that patch of land at the top of our road, where we seem to do doggy introductions. While walking away from her, I gently spoke to her, trying to coax her towards me. Very slowly, she got up and started to move towards me, all the time keeping her body in touch with the hedge. As I waited for her, I could see what an effort she was making; when she reached me she was so pleased with herself and actually wagged her tail. I tried to reassure her, and told her what a good, brave girl she was. I stroked her, and offered her a treat, but at that time, she was too nervous to accept it. When we were sure that Daisy was feeling as confident as possible in this situation, Alan walked back to the house, in order to bring Bentley out to meet Daisy. We had already decided it would be better for Daisy to meet Bentley and Milly one at a time. Daisy was quite nervous, so meeting two new dogs at once, would in my opinion, be very stressful for her. She had already coped with meeting us, and had been travelling in a strange car, to eventually end up somewhere she had never been before, not knowing at all what was going on, or what was going to happen to her. It would be quite un-nerving if that happened to us, wouldn't it? I carried on talking to Daisy in a very calm tone and stroked her gently, I wished there was some way I could definitely let her know that everything was going to be all right. I wished I could make the situation better for her.

I could see Alan approaching with Bentley at his side. A very calm dog, Bentley is able to easily make friends with other dogs; I think he is also able to reassure them. Daisy seemed to tense a little as Bentley came closer. She didn't look at him, but just kept taking sideways glances in order to show him she was not confrontational. Bentley being very adept in canine social skills read the situation immediately. He greeted her in a reassuring manner gently sniffing her, whilst wagging his tail, with that playful look in his facial expression. I'm sure Daisy appreciated his help and concern. First greeting over successfully and Alan left us three together to go and get Milly. Again, this went off without a hitch. Milly, I think, looks to Bentley for guidance, so because he was happy with the situation, so was she. After all the dogs had finished sniffing each other, we set off home. Daisy of course was still very apprehensive about walking in the big outdoors, and especially about crossing the road. For some reason she appeared to feel a little safer when on a grassed area of land as opposed to road or pavement surfaces. I can only think that the grass was familiar to her because of the garden she was let out into in her previous home, and anything else was just so unusual to her, that she would need to go through a learning process about everyday objects and life in general outside of the home. Being alongside Bentley and Milly gave Daisy the confidence to be able to reach that little bit further and take her first steps toward her new home, all be it, wherever possible, staying as close to the hedge as she could get, but at least we tentatively made our way home.

Dogs and humans all went straight into the back garden; we planned to go from there through the door from the garden and into the house, all together. What happened next sounds such a silly little thing, but to me it was an acceptance of the new situation for Daisy, and the feeling that at least she was feeling confident enough with all of us, to relax enough to go to the toilet in the garden. You see I have known of dogs being re-homed, who haven't defecated in their new home environment for a few days because of being so stressed-out, and if that situation doesn't resolve quickly it can lead to medical problems for the dog.

I opened the door that leads from the garden into the house and walked inside, all three dogs followed me as if that was what always happened, and I knew Daisy was going to fit in.

I was interested to see how we would get on in changing Daisy's name. That in its self wouldn't be too difficult, I had done that before, but I'd never been in this situation before; in reality I now had two dogs in the house called Milly!

I felt sorry for Daisy having to learn her new name, especially with having my original Milly around all the time too. I tried not to call original Milly by her name for the time being if I could help it, in order to lessen the confusion for Daisy. That's not quite as easy as it sounds either, well you just do it don't you, so I really had to think about it. I called Daisy's new name as often as possible, every time she approached me I started speaking to her using her name first of all. Then I started calling her to me using her name at the beginning of everything. It was amazing how quickly she understood and responded to her new name. By the end of her first week with us she certainly responded to Daisy when called. Over the next few weeks I gradually began to call original Milly by her name again, at first, of course there were the odd few times when Daisy responded to that name, but that was to be expected, and when it did happen I just ignored it, so Daisy was not getting anything from it, and very shortly she learned not to respond to the word Milly at all.

Over the next few weeks, we all began to know and understand each other. One of the reasons for which Daisy had been re-homed was because her previous family didn't have time to spend with her, to teach her the basic doggy skills associated with being a family pet. Basic training such as sit and down, heelwork on and off the lead, recall, and travelling in the car all had to be patiently taught. Along with that was the task of settling Daisy into the environment around her, such as making her realise the outside world could be fun and she shouldn't be afraid of it. Daisy is very lively and loves to be taught anyway, so is always very eager to go out to the garden and learn. Teaching sit, happened fairly quickly, then down, a little more difficult, but by the end of her second week with us she was proficient in both I had also been clipping a lead to Daisy's collar whilst in the garden and by the end of the third week we were both ready to venture beyond the garden gate. Daisy was still fearful of the unknown, so I decided that if we could get to the end of our road and back, that would be enough to begin with. I was very upbeat hoping to give Daisy the confidence she needed. She was apprehensive but I could tell she wanted to go with me. I opened the gate, went through and Daisy followed me. A car went past and Daisy pulled towards the hedge, she stopped and laid flat to the ground. I coaxed her to her feet, and put myself in-between Daisy and the hedge and walked as far away from it as we could. At least now she stayed on her feet. I took it very slowly; not wanting to push her into something she really didn't have the confidence to do, that would have been wrong, and I think, would have set her back. Her confidence built as each day we went a little further, until eventually we felt confident enough to carry on walking into the village. Although Daisy was doing this, I knew she was very nervous and a little afraid. She was still afraid of traffic noise, although not as much as she had been, but I knew that would be overcome in time. When we reached the centre of the village, people stopped to talk to Daisy, this is a normal occurrence when you're with a Great Dane, people talk to the dog before they talk to you, and most people seem to want to touch a Great Dane too. I'm pleased and proud to say that Daisy took this in her stride, and that these meetings also included other dogs. Once the initial greetings were over Daisy just quietly waited for me move on.

Daisy has an abundance of energy and so very much enjoys learning and joining in with things. I felt Daisy and I would benefit from going to dog training class, not only for the training work, but also for the social aspect too. For the first six months of her life, Daisy hadn't had much exposure to other dogs, people, and everyday life experiences, so I thought going to class would give her a boost, and help her to deal with everyday life in a more confident manner.

I knew of a very good class some miles from our home, run by someone I knew would understand what Daisy was going through. I made arrangements for us to attend, but then realised that Daisy wasn't used to getting in and out of the car, so in turn wasn't used to travelling. I'm lucky enough to have a small driveway at the side of my house which is fenced and gated, and is where I keep the car. I went outside and opened all the doors on the car wide, hopefully making it clear to Daisy there was an escape route if she wanted it. Then, I went back in the house for Daisy, clipped her lead on, and led her out to the car. As we got closer to the car, I encouraged Daisy to get in. She wasn't having it. As we walked up to the car, Daisy turned her body side on to it, refusing to even look at it. I walked her around the outside of the car a few times before taking her back indoors.

I recognised that this task was going to take some time and patience. Daisy would have to feel comfortable and confident enough to get in the car of her own free will. She was still only seven to eight months old, but being a Great Dane, was already the size of a large Labrador or German Shepherd, and there is no way I could lift her in and out. That aside, I never want to force any dog into doing anything they feel apprehensive about, I want them to do it because I ask them to, and they are not afraid. Forcing a dog to do things such as these when they are obviously afraid or not sure, to my mind is bullying, and could lead to problems later. You need plenty of patience and understanding to allow that special bond to form between you and your dog. Don't forget how difficult it must be for the dog, especially if they have been re-homed with you, it's likely they have already formed a bond with someone else. So, what is everyday life to you could be totally alien to the dog.

I tried to imagine what could be going through Daisy's mind. *What did she think I was trying to do; why did I want her to get inside this room on wheels that had brought her here to somewhere she had never known.*

By now, I had realised that Daisy could quite easily be bribed into doing something by offering her food, or encouraging her to play with a toy. Well, these things worked at home but not all the time when we were out and about. So, every morning I opened all the doors on the car as it stood on the drive, then I lined up small pieces of cooked meat right across the inside of the back of the car. They were positioned in such a way that Daisy would actually have to get in the car to be able to retrieve them, and of course she wouldn't feel trapped with all the doors left open for a quick exit.

I took Daisy out to the car and made sure she knew the pieces of meat were in there. Very tentatively, she put her head inside, all the time her nose wriggling like a rabbit, taking in the aroma of the meat. A foot went up onto the edge of the footwell, and I praised her, but she very quickly pulled back. Daisy turned and looked at me with those big brown eyes as if to say, please get that meat for me, I'm scared of going in, but I do want the meat. Next, as Daisy watched, I got into the back of the car, and out the other side, demonstrating to her that there was an escape route. Daisy walked away, so I let her wander around the immediate area freely, sometimes coming to sniff the car, but never going in. With variations, this daily routine carried on for another couple of weeks. I tried bits of all her favourite food, her best-loved toys, and let her watch the other dogs happily getting in and out of the car. Then during the third week, we had a breakthrough. The car, as always, was parked on the drive, all doors wide open, treats positioned strategically inside, when from the corner of my eye, I noticed Daisy actually had her head and shoulders inside the car. She was really stretching to reach the first treat, and only just managed to get it. By now, I was standing close by, and told Daisy what a good girl she was. With hindsight, I should have kept quiet, and waited to see how far Daisy would go, because as soon as she heard me, her head and shoulders made a swift retreat and she came to me. All was not lost though, I reassured her that everything was all right, and then encouraged her to go for the next treat. "Come on," I said, "take it," pointing to the treats in the car. She was hesitant, but along with the head and shoulders her front legs went in the car, then one back foot, with one remaining solidly on the ground. I walked round to the other side of the car, and stood by the open door, calling her to me enthusiastically, to try and encourage her to come right through. I felt elated when Daisy put all four paws down inside the car. She slowly came towards me, picking up each treat on her way, it had worked! I managed to stay calm, hoping to add to Daisy's confidence, and repeated the exercise once more, I didn't want to overdo it, but I did want to make sure it wasn't a one off. Of course, this was just the beginning; there was still a lot of work to do. After a number of days going through this exercise twice a day, I got into the car with Daisy and sat there with her for a few minutes, hoping it would help her to understand that I wanted her to stay there, all done with the doors wide open. Next, it was getting Daisy used to sitting in the car with the doors closed; only one at first, and when I knew she was comfortable with that, the others followed one by one, until the last one was closed behind her when she got in. After that came the short drives, just round the block at first, and then short journeys of a few miles. I wanted to show Daisy that when she went out in the car we sooner or later would return home.

It may seem a tedious task to you, but well worth doing in Daisy's own time. It gave her more confidence in me, and herself, and once she actually set foot inside the car, things moved on pretty quickly. From the two and a half weeks it actually took her to first set foot in the car, it was probably just over another week to reach the stage where when I told her to get in the car, she did so, and she soon learned to lie down comfortably, and enjoy the drive. Some dogs never have a problem with getting in a car, and not all will take the time Daisy did, to get used to it, some may take longer. All I'm saying is be considerate in all aspects of training, be patient, and help their confidence in you, to grow; it's well worth it in the long run.

One of our initial outings was just a matter of a ten to fifteen-minute drive to our vet's. I wanted to order an ID tag for Daisy, so took her along for the experience. On arrival, I parked the car, noticing that the surgery didn't appear to be very busy. As I opened the car door for Daisy, I told her to wait, so that I was able to get hold of her lead. I try to teach this to all my dogs, it could be the difference between avoiding an accident or them stepping out into the path of another vehicle. Grasping the lead, I said "OK, come," Daisy got out and stood by my side. We walked into an empty waiting room, and two veterinary nurses came through from the back. They thought we had come to see a vet, and told us the surgery wasn't on at the moment, hence the empty waiting room. I told them we only wanted to order an ID tag, and that Daisy was here for the experience. One of the nurses made a fuss of Daisy whist the other took down the details for the tag. I asked if it was all right for me and Daisy to have a stroll round outside, as part of Daisy's training, the nurses agreed, and Daisy and I went outside. There's a small grassed area with a few trees on it, for visiting dogs to relieve themselves if need be, and on the other side beyond a small wooden fence is a small field, with some sheep in it, and on that particular day, a small pony too. Mindful of all the animals involved, I walked Daisy towards the fence. My aim is to encourage Daisy to accept any animal, and to be at ease in most situations. Daisy had seen sheep before, and showed no reaction to them, then she noticed the pony, and the pony noticed us. Daisy tensed her body, and frowned – like

Bentley, she has a very expressive face – she made a very low, very quiet sort of rumbling sound. It wasn't aggressive, it was more of a *I'm not sure what this is* or *what I'm supposed to do* sort of sound. I told her to be quiet, and that it was all right, and kept a comfortable distance between us for all concerned. Daisy was very good, and didn't make another sound; she also stood perfectly still and let the pony take a good look at her. I felt very proud of her, and took this as a sign of her growing trust in me. The two vet nurses came out to take the pony back to the stable block. Daisy and I, backed up, and kept a safe distance. We didn't know how the pony would react to being so close to us, and I didn't want to push Daisy either. The nurses walked the pony past us, Daisy watched it all the time, but she didn't make a sound, and stood perfectly still.

Now to get back in the car, I opened the door, and gestured toward the inside. I gave a very slight gentle tug on the lead, and told Daisy to "Get in". She didn't get in, I remember thinking, well what am I going to do now, there's no way I could lift her in. I told myself to be positive. Daisy had got into the car with no trouble whilst we were at home, so there's no reason why she can't now. I got into the car clutching Daisy's lead; I tugged the lead ever so slightly towards me and spoke words of encouragement. It worked; she got in and settled down, then looked at me as if to say, 'only joking'. I knew there were bound to be one or two minor hiccups to come, but generally this exercise was a success.

Tinkerbell

The postman delivered Daisy's ID tag a few days after I had ordered it. I unpacked it, and showed it to her, pointing out to her that the other dogs had these attached to their collars. After she had inspected it, I attached it to her collar for her. The moment she moved of course, there was a tinkling sound as the tag bounced against the other metal parts of her collar. Daisy obviously hadn't had this experience before and looked quite comical as she turned her head this way, and that, the way dogs do when they are trying to work something out. I pointed out to her that the noise was coming from her collar as she moved. After a few more motions of the head, ending in Daisy cocking her head to one side, she appeared to accept this, and happily ran off down the garden to join the others.

My three-dog household is coming together nicely. All the dogs enjoy playing together, and although it is Milly and Daisy who play together the most, I have noticed that even Bentley is playing a little more, and enjoys a good game with young Daisy. For a seven-year-old Great Dane this is good. He runs up and down the garden, doing his little twirls as he goes along, with Daisy at his side.

Since Daisy arrived, all the dogs have been tired, and ready for their beds by mid-evening; it's a bit like having toddlers in the house, playing all day long, then settling down after their evening meal, and going to sleep to regenerate ready for another long day of happy play.

Now that getting in the car is no longer a problem for Daisy, it's time we attended training class. We were the first to arrive at the church hall where the class was held, and took our place at the far end of the room. As the others arrived Daisy started to tense, but overall I think she was very brave and did very well. We were able to do sit, and down, and began to socialise a little. These meetings can be stressful at first for the dog, who after all has no idea why we are there, and on top of keeping an eye on all the other dogs around them are being asked to do tasks in a strange place for all the world to see. Not to mention their human companion being stressed and transferring this to their dog. We tried walking to heel in the hall, and although Daisy does this outside she began to pull a bit in class. It was a bit frustrating but I knew she would settle down eventually – it was her first time here. We also tried recall but Daisy was a little distracted by the new environment. Towards the end of the meeting, Anne, the trainer in charge, brought out an agility tunnel, some of the other young dogs who had been attending a while got excited at the sight. They really enjoyed running through the tunnel from one end to the other, and barked excitedly. Daisy had a good look and sniff at the tunnel, and you could tell she did really want a go, but just wasn't quite sure. We tried to get her to just put her head in, using pieces of meat - but she couldn't just yet. I was very proud of what she had achieved, we drove home happy and looking forward to next week's session. Daisy and I practiced every day for next Thursdays training class, so when she started her first season on the Wednesday it was quite disappointing. I knew this would be on its way and it had to happen but it would have been nice to get through our six weeks training first. Training class would have to be put on hold for the duration.

Daisy's story wouldn't be complete without first telling you about her eye.

Before I met Daisy in the flesh, I had seen some photographs of her. On those pictures, I had noticed that her left eye looked runny. I had concerns for her, and thought it may be something like inward growing eyelids. I had never actually seen this before, but had read enough books to be aware of it. After talking to the family she was living with at that time, they made arrangements to take Daisy to see the vet during the morning of the same day of my visit, which would be later that afternoon.

The vet had told the family, Daisy's runny eye was probably some kind of allergy/conjunctivitis, caused by seasonal changes, the season then being spring/early summer, so it could be something like hayfever, and had prescribed some drops to be put into her eye. Of course when I took Daisy home with me I administered the drops as prescribed, and the eye, although still a little runny, began to greatly improve. Unfortunately, shortly after the drops were finished, Daisy's eye became as runny as ever again. I took Daisy to my vet, and that's where we were given the diagnosis of entropion; to explain this, the following has been taken from; *Veterinary Notes For Dog Owners*, 2002, edited by Trevor Turner Bvet Med, MRCVS.

Entropion. It is due to an excess of eyelid tissue, or a small eye, or both. The result being that varying amounts of hair covered eyelid can turn in to rub directly against the cornea or conjunctiva, or both. It is usually extremely painful, and the damage caused to the cornea can render the eye blind. Most dogs are affected by the age of six months. Occasionally the condition is self-correcting as the puppy grows but in the vast majority of affected dogs, surgery is necessary, to turn the eyelid away from the surface of the eye. This is usually successful, but surely as with other inherited problems, it would be better if dog breeders try to avoid producing this condition in their stock.

And I can't agree more. I just want Daisy to be better. She must feel soreness and irritation in her eye, but she never complains or gives the slightest clue there is anything wrong at all. Daisy is such a love; she enjoys every day, and makes the most of everything. She deserves, like all dogs, to have a happy, loving, and pain free life, so the sooner the eye is operated on, the better. The operation was scheduled for a couple of days after our initial visit, in the mean time we had been sent home with some more eye drops. These would help soothe and protect the eye from damage.

The morning of the operation, Daisy and I travelled to the surgery. I hated to leave her there, but knew it was for the best. Poor Daisy; in a matter of just a few weeks, she had found herself in a different environment, in a new home, had started her first season, and was now having an eye operation.

I went home, but couldn't relax, I wanted the phone to ring and the vet to say everything had gone to plan, and that I could go and pick Daisy up, and bring her back home to us. That phone call came later that afternoon, and I couldn't get to the car quick enough. The short ten to fifteen-minute drive to the vets seemed to take forever. When I did arrive at the surgery, it was very busy, anxiety built within me, the minutes I waited felt like hours. Eventually a veterinary nurse came towards me; I had handed Daisy over to her that morning so she knew why I was there. The nurse went through the door into the back of the building where the operations and treatments were carried out. Presently the door opened again and the nurse was walking towards me again, only this time Daisy was walking behind her, in an unsteady fashion, and still slightly sedated from the operation. As soon as Daisy had me in her sight, she wagged her tail as vigorously as the effects of the anaesthetic would allow, and lumbered towards me. I must say it's quite a shock coming face to face with your dog, who has just had eye surgery. Daisy had a line of stitches at the corner of her left eye, which was also very swollen, adding to that, she was also wearing one of those *lamp shade* collars round her neck, to stop her scratching her eye, or rubbing the side of her face on the floor. Small dogs can have problems moving around when wearing one of those, never mind a Great Dane, but at least she was not yet fully grown, the collar was so wide I wasn't sure if she would get through the house door with it on, never mind get in the car. It wasn't going to be practical, but we would manage somehow. For now, all I wanted to do was get Daisy home and comfort her. I managed to steer Daisy out to the car, but there was no way she could get in with the collar on, so I took it off, then put it back on once she was laying down in the car, going through the same routine, but in reverse, once we reached home. I took her into the house, and then replaced the collar before bringing the other dogs into the room to greet her. I had made a bed for Daisy in the dining room – Hugo's Hospital; she could rest properly in there without being disturbed by the others, and of course initially sleep off the effects of the anaesthetic. The day after Daisy was a little quiet but more like her, then each day she became more boisterous, and just wanted to play. I was pleased really because that meant she wasn't too bothered about her eye, but my problem was trying to keep her calm and quiet as the vet had instructed. Although the area around the eye was swollen and the stitches looked quite sore, it wasn't long before it all healed, and Daisy obviously felt comfortable, with that, and her first season out of the way, we were ready to re-join the training class.

Although Daisy is nervous in the training class, I think she is doing really well, and being nervous doesn't stop her from enjoying herself. She gets a bit tense when we do group exercises, but is becoming more confident. I smile to myself when we do food refusal, because I can sense Daisy really wants to take the treat, especially when it's a bit of cooked ham or chicken, but shows great self-control and doesn't eat the food until told to do so. You may be surprised to learn that Daisy's favourite thing we do in class is crawling through the agility tunnel.

Ann brings out the tunnel at the end of each season, it's something most of the dogs love, and there is always an air of excitement and excited barks when the tunnel appears. All the dogs wait their turn, watching enthusiastically as each dog takes its place at the mouth of the tunnel. This particular week, our third or fourth, I think, Daisy, as ever was watching tentatively. Then came her turn. I positioned her at one end of the tunnel, and Ann, was at the exit end with some juicy pieces of meat. I could tell Daisy was ready to go, but expected her to just run along the length of the tunnel towards Ann. To my delight Daisy actually went inside the tunnel, quickly crawled through, then emerged triumphantly out the other end, where Ann gave her the meat. Everyone in class cheered, they all knew of Daisy's struggle, and what an achievement something like this meant to her. I think Daisy picked up on this excitement, because then she went back in the tunnel and out the other side at least another half dozen times, before running to my side, sitting facing me and looking at me with those big brown eyes as though saying, "Well aren't I a good girl?" "Come on then where's my treat?"

It's now November, Daisy has been with us for six months, and she is now twelve months old. She is always full of beans, and has really changed our household. I liken her to an overactive child who never stops. She is on the go all day long; training, going for walks, playing with the other dogs, and or toys, running round the house and garden, generally enjoying herself, doing what most young dogs do, given the chance. The thing is because of her size, everything seems ten times as manic!

Her eye has settled down now, and doesn't bother her at all, and like most Great Dane's she enjoys being in the company of the family, and joining in everyday life; so much so, it took me three and a half hours to write one and a half pages on the computer today. She wanted to see what I was doing, and wanted my attention, so when I tried to concentrate she kept getting into mischief, things like taking Alan's boots out into the garden and leaving them somewhere out there. She doesn't chew them up, but likes to carry them about, and put them in her bed, or just play with them for a little while. Then when he comes to put them on, they're all soggy.

Bentley, Milly, and Daisy truly are valued members of our household. Each is an individual, but all share their lives with us, enjoying a relationship built on mutual trust, respect, and compassion.

At the time of writing this book, during the opening years of the twenty first century, I believe our canine companions are very much misunderstood.

Dogs are still the same as they have always been, being very adept in picking up the thoughts, feelings, and words of their human companions. But the mutual understanding, and compassion, between dog, and human, that was forged thousands of years ago, seems to have got lost in time.

Society in general has become less sociable, and this in turn, has had an effect on our dogs.

In my opinion, dogs and people are supposed to live alongside each other, supporting each other through a relationship based on trust, compassion, and understanding.